FROM MANY ONE

A book based on lectures delivered at Pomona College, Claremont, California, in March 1947 under the Joseph Horsfall Johnson Foundation.

FROM MANY
ONE

The Process of Political Integration
The Problem of World Government

CRANE BRINTON

231308

GREENWOOD PRESS, PUBLISHERS
WESTPORT, CONNECTICUT

PREFACE

This essay was developed from a series of three lectures delivered at Pomona College in the spring of 1947. The subject is an enormous one and it is of course not really covered here. My purpose has been to point out what seems to me a field of study as yet inadequately cultivated — the objective study of just how human beings do come together in territorially larger political units, the study of the process of political integration. This book does but raise certain questions, to which the research of the social scientist ought to provide some sort of answers.

In its first form, the book goes back to a brief paper on "Some Historical Precedents for the Integration of Political Units" which I gave in the autumn of 1946 as part of a conference on "The Development of International Society," fifth in the series of Bicentennial Conferences at Princeton University. I wish here to thank the authorities in charge of the Princeton Bicentennial Conferences for affording me the opportunity to present this paper.

In their next form, these chapters were given as lectures under the Joseph Horsfall Johnson Foundation at Pomona College in the spring of 1947. I am pleased to report my Claremont audiences were very far from passive. In the course of a delightful and very busy week I discussed the problems raised herein with all sorts of groups, formal and informal. I have an especially vivid memory of a two-hour session with the undergraduate world federationists, from which I at least learned much. I have not altered the fundamental point of view with which I approached the subject of these lectures, but in many ways their final form bears the mark of the coöperation of my Pomona friends — though I hasten to add that none of them should be held to blame for what is here printed. I should like to add my thanks to President E. Wilson Lyon and the authorities of Pomona College for inviting me to give the lectures, and for their help in securing their publication. Here again, I must insist that the opinions and value-judgments expressed in this book are my own, and are in no sense the responsibility of Pomona College.

For help in preparing the manuscript I should like to thank my colleagues, Professors Donald McKay and Myron Gilmore, my secretary, Miss Elizabeth F. Hoxie; and for listening patiently, critically, and most usefully, my wife.

Crane Brinton

Peacham, Vermont
September 1947

CONTENTS

INTRODUCTION

INTRODUCTION

This book is an attempt to set my own mind straight on matters of the very gravest importance. It is elementary, perhaps even naïve; but the fundamental problem with which it is concerned stands in need of the kind of stripping and simplification innocence — even acquired innocence — can give it. The problem is exceedingly familiar; many of us concerned in word or deed with public affairs are obsessed with it. I think it came home to me personally in the most acute form when a colleague, a physical scientist of great distinction, said to me, "We physical scientists have now succeeded in devising a way — several ways — to destroy the human race; you social scientists have got to find a way to keep the human race from using the opportunity we have given it." Now my colleague's remark was in no sense unusual; in one form or another it has been made many times since the bomb fell on Hiroshima, and indeed, perhaps since the bow and arrow first supplemented the war club. I had no profound answer ready, and could only make a flippant and, I am sure, annoying answer: "Then the human race is done for."

Shallow, hasty, and flippant though that answer was, I cannot after long and exceedingly sober reflection bring myself to believe that any other answer is possible, granted the question is put, as the scientist put it, in the form of the dilemma: find a way to stop war or perish. *I do not personally believe that the human race faces any such dilemma. The formula "either . . . or," never very realistic, gets less and less so as the problems it attempts to state get more and more complex and generalized. In spite of the atomic bomb and the even more horrible possibilities rumored of "biological" warfare, I think that there will be another general war and that the human race will survive it. When there will be such a war, and between whom it will be fought, I could not even bring myself to guess.*

Teachers, preachers, educators, even politicians, are telling the growing generation that there must be no war, and that therefore there will be no war. I have doubts as to whether this is wise teaching and to these doubts I shall revert in a brief concluding word. This book, however, is not concerned with the whole of the associated set of problems involved in my scientific colleague's stated dilemma: world peace or world ruin. It is rather an indication of some of the questions a conscientious social scientist must ask if he really wishes to try to apply the methods of the scientist to the study of the problem of modern war. This is not the place to attempt to discuss the methods and limitations of the so-called social sciences.[1]

[1] I have given very brief consideration to this problem in the first chapter of my *Anatomy of Revolution* (Norton, 1938).

I shall not attempt very great generalizations of the sort produced by Henry and Brooks Adams and by almost any philosopher of history. I am not looking for the relation between the second law of thermodynamics, or the Einstein formula, and the fate of man. Nor shall I — I trust — repeat the commonplaces of common sense and professional caution about the lessons of history.

In between the grand views of the philosopher and the petty views of the historical craftsman I should like to find a middle way, much as natural science found such a middle way between philosopher and technician. I should like to see how far I could modestly justify my friend the physical scientist's kindly assumption that the social scientist has something to contribute. That contribution can be no magic solution, no final end to the evil of war. Mankind may yet find salvation even here on earth, but not through science, physical or social — not, at any rate, through science alone.

All the social scientist can do is to indicate strong probabilities. He can never be certain, and he can never be possessed — not even by the Truth. Now,

Lyman Bryson's recent *Science and Freedom* (Columbia University Press, 1947) is a suggestive essay. The interested reader can find helpful suggestions for further reading on this vast and confused subject of what the social sciences amount to in the Selective Reading List by Ronald Thompson in *Theory and Practice in Historical Study* (Bulletin 54, Social Science Research Council, 1946).

in this matter of war and peace, the social scientist can begin with an extremely strong probability that what common sense calls peace on this earth can be kept for long periods of time only within the boundaries of a single organized state exercising the kind of authority we associate with a legal system, with an administrative system, with a police force. This is a generalization from some five thousand years of written history. The agitators for world federation are almost certainly right: no world peace without some form of world government. Treaties, alliances, leagues, united nations, and any other device for bringing sovereign states together have never yet kept them together.

It would seem, then, that those who wish to promote the cause of peace should study carefully the ways in which governments able to keep peace within a given area have been set up, and above all the ways in which such governments have been able to extend the areas within which peace obtains. For it is a commonplace of history that such areas have been very considerably extended. They have never included the whole world, nor even what we of Western society somewhat immodestly call in historical writing the "known world." But union of once independent states, the process I shall call "political integration," has occurred, and seems to me worth the closest attention of all who wish to promote the cause of peace.

The process has by no means been neglected by students of human relations. I make no claim to break new ground in this brief book, which rests on a considerable body of historical work. But I do maintain that precisely the kind of people who ought to put their minds to the concrete realities of the problem of political integration — that is, the earnest workers, young and old, who in this country are trying to strengthen the United Nations into a World Government — have not generally done so. It is to them above all that the following chapters are addressed, not to discourage them, but to encourage them.

Many of the world federationists, of course, neglect the study of the actual methods by which political unions have been achieved because they are convinced that the past has been so hopelessly bad that we can learn nothing good from it. This attitude, which is a common one among revolutionists and enthusiasts of all kinds, must always be pretty much unaffected by the kind of evidence I am here trying to bring forward. But many of the enthusiasts for world federation now seem to me to be contemptuous of the experience of the race outside the United States for another and slightly different reason. These may perhaps be more willing to look at the record. Briefly, I think they are, in spite of all that has gone on since 1787, overimpressed with the success of the American Constitution. Here was a union produced, apparently, by talk-

ing, thinking, document-editing and document-signing. Here was something new *and* planned. *And it worked. Why not plan further, for the world union?*

Of course we should so plan. But we should never forget — what any good farmer knows — that there may be all sorts of gaps between plans and results. Americans might think of the Eighteenth Amendment as well as of the original Constitution. Both have probably been overdone as propaganda examples, the Eighteenth Amendment by conservatives and pessimists, the Constitution by innovators and optimists. The relation between law-making (or treaty-making or constitution-making) and actual reform of human behavior is a complex and continuous one. Real reform, it has been said, does not begin with a law, but ends with a law. This is as false as its opposite, the belief that if you can only make a law (or international agreement) you have effected a real reform of human behavior. Sensible people know that neither extreme holds in this world.

Nevertheless, in the balance, it seems to me that many educated Americans, and especially Americans interested in world affairs, tend rather to the extreme of reliance on getting a law passed — a law as "advanced" as they possibly can get. And since our reformers often show as much skill as the wicked and corrupt do at the ways of pressure politics, they often get very advanced laws passed. Now I do not think there is much chance that any of our American world federationists can by any kind of propaganda and pressure-group tactics get signed, sealed, and delivered a charter or constitution setting up a world-state. Should they against all odds succeed in doing so, I should expect the failure of this charter to work to be at least as complete as the failure of the Eighteenth Amendment. Spectacular failures are bad for the morale of the faithful. The atom bomb is not the only danger we face.

It would seem probable that in international affairs, as in other kinds of human relations, overambitious, premature and "unrealistic" planning and chartering is bound to lead to failure. It is because I believe that international relations can be improved, that we can get longer breathing spells of peace, that we may even in some ways regulate wars, that we shall almost certainly get increasing political integration among hitherto "independent" states, that I am against an attempt now to create a true world government of a true world-state. Or at the very least, I should, before I joined the movement for world federation, want answers for some of the questions I raise in the following chapters.

THE ANCIENT WORLD

I

THE ANCIENT WORLD

It is only a bit over a century ago that Jeremy Bentham coined the word "international." Yet ever since the beginnings of our Western society in the Nile and Euphrates valleys there have been the kind of organized relations among formal political units Bentham wished to designate by the word "international." The units — whether they are called tribes, or city-states, or kingdoms, or nations — have combined in a bewildering variety of alliances and leagues, have made treaties and broken them, have waged war and patched up peace. I do not propose in this book any such ambitious aim as the ordering of five millenniums of international relations into some neat evolutionary pattern from which we can all take heart for the future. Nor can I, for lack of competence in these fields, make use of the stores of experience in such matters available in the past of China, India, and other lands which were until recent times outside our Western society.

I propose more modestly to take a few samples, widely spaced in time and place, of one phase of international relations — the union of what were formerly separate, independent, and hence war-making political units into a greater unit. Once this greater unit has been achieved, though within it there may well be occasional mob violence, crime, even perhaps what we call civil war, the conventional, the customary sort of war we are all familiar with becomes impossible. This process of making from many one I shall call, in whatever fashion it is achieved, the process of political integration. It seems to me that today, when some of our more thoughtful, and most of our more excited public figures are urging that the United Nations, which is no more than a voluntary league, be somehow made into a supranational government and state, we may at least learn something of the concrete problems of such an enterprise from efforts made in the past to integrate independent political units into a larger "sovereign" whole.

Yet such a proposal unavoidably brings up a question I am afraid we can by no means agree in answering — that is, the question of the validity in such matters of an appeal to what are rather wistfully called the lessons of history. I am very anxious not to enter at this point on a debate with you or with myself on the uses and limitations of history. Some of you, I expect, agree with the aphorism that all we learn from history is that we learn nothing from history, and I must confess that in my gloomier moments I find some truth in the aphorism. But the subject would require a longer book than this, and I shall have to content myself with the flat statement that if we believe at all in the objective scientific study of human relations we must hold that an adequate understanding of such relations in the past will, other things being equal, provide at least a kind of formsheet for our guidance in the present.

You have perhaps noted the introduction of two cautious, face-saving, and not unambiguous phrases — "adequate" and that old academic favorite, "other things being equal." By "adequate" I mean that in any one specific instance there be sufficient accurate information so that the determining variables in the situation can be isolated for analysis and their relative importance roughly weighed; and by "other things being equal" I mean that in our contemporary problem — in this case the building of a world government as an extension of, or in place of, the United Nations — there be no new major variables.

As to the first difficulty, I think we do not yet have information adequate for more than most tentative conclusions as to how the process of political integration has been worked out in the past, though I hope that, as historians turn more to sociological and psychological problems, they can add vastly to our store of reliable and relevant facts. At any rate, I shall not in this book pretend to do more than sketch some very tentative first approximations, and for these I believe our supply of facts is adequate, though barely so.

As for the second difficulty, I am quite willing to grant that there may be new factors, or old factors so altered as to be unrecognizable. These new factors may make useless any attempt to apply to the problems of today what we can learn, for instance, of the way in which the hundreds of tribes and city-states of the ancient world were made into the one Roman Empire. But surely the burden of pointing out the existence of these new factors should lie with those who deny the validity for us today of what our ancestors, distant and immediate, have gone through? In my last chapter I shall say something about what some of these new factors might be; but I must confess that I am, perhaps from professional prejudice, very skeptical indeed about the possibilities of great and striking novelties in human dealings with other human beings. Let us have the courage to face commonplaces: the new world-state will not be built in a day, just because "Rome wasn't built in a day." No doubt the drama of history is made for the most part by those who are impatient of recorded history; but the impatient are by no means always the free, and they rarely do the real work of this world.

And yet, before I take the old academic road back to Greece and Rome, I owe you the acknowledgment that perhaps the journey will not repay us. It may just possibly be that we are now in the midst of times when men can change as they have never changed before. Habits, loyalties, institutions may under the extraordinary pressures of the last few years prove more fluid, more pliable, more yielding to the plans of virtuous men than they ever have been in human experience, much as the behavior of quite ordinary physical things changes under the extraordinarily high temperatures or high pressures we can now produce in the laboratory. I shall, for instance, have much to say about the way in which that nexus of habits, emotions, and ideas we call patriotism, or more coldly, nationalism, has persisted in countries like Ireland and Poland. I shall conclude that what we call nationalism is for any reasonable period in our times a constant, not to be stamped out by conquest, nor even to be exorcised by professorial and editorial incantations. I shall not, I trust, be guilty of such innocence as is expressed in the tiresome — and inaccurate — platitude that "human nature doesn't change"; but I shall assume that five thousand years of history tell us pretty accurately within what limits human behavior changes, how fast it changes, and how permanently. This assumption may be false in 1948. If so, my caution will seem silly, my attempt at detachment vain, and my whole enterprise pretty pointless. This, however, is the risk anyone takes who attempts prognosis in human relations — or shall I say frankly, prophecy.

II

The five millenniums since the first civilized states of our Western society arose in the Near East have witnessed the rise and fall of many states. There have been times when there was a very great number indeed of separate and more or less "sovereign" political units, as in the great days of the Greek city-state and in the period of feudal disintegration at the beginning of the Middle Ages. There has been one period, briefer than we always realize, when, with the exception of a few half-savage Germanic and Slavic tribes, the whole of "our" world made but a single state. The Roman Empire was a real world-state, since most of Asia and Africa, and all of America and Oceania, were literally other worlds. For the most part, however, this Western world of ours has been divided into competing states, big, little, and middle-sized, kept in that most unstable equilibrium we call the balance of power. You have only to open the pages of Thucydides to see that most of the concepts we all apply to current international relations apply to the Peloponnesian War. The scale is smaller — indeed these city-states must seem almost Lilliputian to us — but the thoughts and feelings of their citizens are essentially the same, right through to the question of war-guilt. In Greece, too, the other nation was to blame. You will recall that passage in Thucydides in which he explains how the

Spartans reproached the Athenians with the original act of blasphemy which moved the gods to set in train the irrepressible conflict; and how the Athenians in turn reproached the Spartans with a sacrilege so shocking to the gods that it had to be properly punished by a good sound war.

There was the same desire for peace, for some way to transcend the limitations of the independent city-state. There is, for example, that pathetic passage from *Lysistrata* in which the heroine urges that the subject city-states of the Athenian Empire be united in a genuine common citizenship, and uses a metaphor of weaving:

> Then you should card it and comb it and mingle it all
> in one basket of love and of unity,
> Citizens, visitors, strangers and sojourners — all the entire, undivided community.
>
> . . . . .
>
> These to one mighty political aggregate tenderly, carefully, gather and pull;
> Twining them all in one thread of good fellowship thence a magnificent bobbin to spin,
> Weaving a garment of comfort and dignity, worthily wrapping the people therein.

Well, the garment was indeed woven, though not of the softest wool, and perhaps not by the best weaver. Not long after Aristophanes wrote, Philip of Macedon and his son united Greece — or enslaved it — and a few generations later the Romans were able to finish the job. The time came when, as Lysistrata had wanted, the men of Athens no longer fought against the men of Sparta, nor, indeed, as men of Athens, fought at all. The quarreling city-states of Greece had been integrated into the Roman province of Achaia.

What we are concerned with here is the process by which once "independent" or "sovereign" states yield, voluntarily or involuntarily, that independence or sovereignty to some other political grouping. Yet since the word "sovereignty" is a notably complex word, charged with centuries of debates among political philosophers, and since the process as above outlined sounds a bit mechanical, I should like to translate it into the language of human emotions. *Dulce et decorum est pro patria mori.* We can say that we are about to study some of the ways in which the areas within which and for which it is sweet and fitting to die, and kill, have changed. For, of course, they have changed, and often with a rapidity which shows how wrong are those who deny the reality of historical change in human behavior. I suppose many Virginians still do not like Yankees, and no doubt the converse is true; but I take it that Virginians no longer feel that it is sweet and fitting to kill Yankees that Virginia may live.

Purely for purposes of analysis, one may distinguish between two different ways of achieving the union of separate political units into a single one. There is the process in which a single unit conquers or tricks other units into defeat and absorption; thus unit A will swallow units B, C, D, and so on to produce a greater unit A. This I shall call the method of imperialism. And there is the process by which a number of units get together voluntarily and agree to merge themselves in a larger whole; thus A, B, C, and D will unite to form E. This I shall call the method of federalism. Now imperialism and federalism are in these senses mere abstract polar concepts, useful to us in ordering our thought, but by no means accurate descriptions of how political units do get integrated. Pure force or pure consent, pure imperialism or pure federalism, simply do not exist on this planet. The conqueror always finds among the conquered some who had been won to his cause in advance. To use the language of our own times, there have always been quislings. Nor does the best of federal unions evolve from unanimous consent and without frustrations. It would clearly be an exaggeration to say that when at long last the State of Rhode Island and Providence Plantations deigned to join our federal union force was required to bring her in; but I think we can say that at least force of circumstances was necessary to that end.

One further general observation, and I shall be ready to attempt the analysis of a concrete instance of political integration. In the record of our Western society, instances of federal union are very few indeed, fewer than most of us Americans, who enjoy the fruits of one of these rare unions, always realize. They can be counted on the fingers — the Achaean and the Aetolian Leagues in ancient Greece, the United Provinces, known to the outside world from the strongest of them as Holland, and Switzerland. To these must no doubt be added the British Commonwealth of Nations and the Union of Socialist Soviet Republics, both of which certainly have federal elements. Domestically Canada, Australia, and South Africa are very interesting examples of federal practice. But the British Commonwealth as a whole, and probably the USSR as a whole, are rather extreme examples, the first of a unit that looks like a congeries, held together by a bond so apparently tenuous as to seem juridically hardly a bond at all, and the second of a unit composed of juridically autonomous units, but actually governed by a strongly centralized group in the Kremlin. I do not wish to enter here into the controversial question of the reality of Russian federalism. I suspect it is not so unreal as Mr. Kravchenko says it is, nor so real as Mr. Corliss Lamont says it is. But we haven't at present a chance to get at the real facts. Both the British Empire and the Russian Empire are at any rate examples of successful political integration of separate territorial units; and it is to be hoped that objective social scientists can one day study them both in full freedom, for both are in a sense working experiments in the transcending of the parochial nation-state.

These British and Russian experiments, and others going on today, like the French experiment with their Negro dependents in Africa, are more likely to help in the problem of world union than will our own American experiment. For, great achievement though the American melting pot of races now seems to be, successful though we have been in absorbing in a surprising unity individuals from the very same peoples who war so fiercely in Europe, the melting-pot solution is clearly not one that can be generally adopted. Even the wholesale movement of armies and workers as between France and Germany in the last six years made no beginning of melting French and Germans into a single people.

Most political integration, however, has been achieved by what I call the method of imperialism. The Roman Empire grew around the conquering Roman legions: France — as we shall see an excellent example of the integration of many units into one — was built up by soldiers, diplomatists, feudal lawyers, administrators in the service of the Crown of France. Force, guile, and some lucky marriages, rather than what we think of as voluntary consent, made modern France out of a feudal congeries.

Yet if force has in the past usually begun the process of political integration, no abiding new unit has ever

been held together by force alone. Federalism, the
method of consent, creeps into the imperialistically
built state, if only in the disguise of habit and tradition. The most successful of empires, the Roman and
the British, afford mixtures of force and consent which
are bewildering to the numerous simple souls who see
politics in the hard clear lines of right and wrong. The
Roman Republic fought a war to deny to her Italian
allies the right to insist on Roman citizenship for
themselves, and having beaten them in the field in the
Social War proceeded to grant them all Roman citizenship. The British have killed for Empire, but they
have also freed for Commonwealth. Force alone is
good for nothing but raids, like those of Attila; something more than force — custom, law, administrative
regularity at least part way down the road to government by consent — is necessary to the most tyrannical
of imperial states.

III

You will remember that Gibbon declared that "if a
man were called to fix the period in the history of the
world, during which the condition of the human race
was most happy and prosperous, he would, without
hesitation, name that which elapsed from the death
of Domitian to the accession of Commodus." To our
Victorian forefathers, secure in peace, Gibbon's ideal

on earth seemed stodgy, unaspiring, not nearly so interesting to contemplate as exciting ages like those of the *Chanson de Roland* or the *Morte d'Arthur,* when knighthood was in flower. I am not so sure but that in 1948 we are more inclined to agree with Gibbon. At any rate, the years he chose, 96 A.D. to 180 A.D., mark the nearest to "one world" at peace we Westerners have ever seen realized in institutions on this earth. It is true that toward the North and East barbaric groups of German, Slavic, and Hunnic stocks were constantly pressing upon the *cordon sanitaire* held against them by the Roman legions. It is true that slavery, suffering, and all the rest of the tale of human woes is no briefer here than at any other time in human history. It may well be true that Antonine Rome was already a state in decline, a society that had failed to resolve fundamental social and economic tensions which must at least be mitigated if a society is to endure. Nevertheless, Antonine Rome did preserve international peace for a longer time and over a greater area than any other political organization Western man has ever set up. The Roman Empire at its height was our greatest Western international society.

The Empire was built up basically in the days of the Republic, and on the whole by force of arms. I cannot quite accept the extension to Roman imperial expansion of the explanation of British imperial expansion which attributes that extraordinary process to a fit of absence of mind. (Indeed, I cannot quite accept this as an explanation of *British* expansion.) Granted that, especially in the earlier days, Roman leaders were clearly not aiming at world dominion, granted that Roman involvements in the Near East seem at first hesitating and uncertain, it is clear that by the time of Julius Caesar and the triumvirs we are dealing with self-conscious big shots who knew what they wanted at least as well as did Napoleon or Hitler. Unlike these last, some of the Romans got what they wanted — world rule.

It is worth noting also that, though the process by which in the course of some four centuries the several thousand "independent" city-states, tribes, kingdoms, and other political units of the Mediterranean world were integrated into larger units is not absolutely regular, there is a marked general tendency for the number of these units to diminish after each major crisis of war. The victorious swallow a few of the vanquished; rarely, very rarely, some of the conquered come together in a genuine federal state. Finally, as the era of the triumvirs approaches, we find a most unstable balance of power, and therefore constant wars, among relatively few great territorial states and their satellites — Rome, Carthage, Macedonia, Egypt, Syria. I do not really think I am being false to my training as a professional historian — a training which makes one shy off from possible anachronisms — if I roundly describe those last few centuries before Christ as an era of "superpowers."

We cannot here attempt at length the interesting task of analyzing by what skills and by what strokes of fortune the Romans won out over their competitors. These skills were clearly not solely the technical skills of successful warfare. They were in part also political skills, which we understand much less well than we do the simpler skills of fighting. The Romans — at any rate the Romans who got into what we may call the colonial service — were not idealists; they felt themselves pretty superior on the whole to the natives, even when the natives were countrymen of Plato and Aristotle; they were probably — though this really is a rather shocking guess for a historian to make — not even very intelligent. I mean, they probably would not come out very high in a modern scholastic aptitude test. They were not, in fact, very much like the kind of people who nowadays are agitating for a world government and a superstate. Yet they succeeded where the brighter Greeks and the more enterprising Carthaginians failed. If you wish to learn more about their methods, you should go to Polybius, and to the *Discourses* of Machiavelli, where you will see by example how much more than Dublin conferences, Humber resolutions, college lectures, and books on *The Anatomy of Peace* is needed to make of many states one.

I shall here attempt, not a dynamic account of the building up of the Empire, but rather a static analysis of what seems to have held it together. At the apex of the structure was the Emperor, the Caesar. Fairly early in the history of the Empire, we find him deified. This deification of the emperors was long a puzzle to modern historians. They were inclined to attribute it in the main to the megalomaniac ambition of the individual emperors, deprived as they were of the chastening virtues of a free society. Actually many of the emperors found being a god rather uncomfortable, and put up with it out of a sense of duty. For the deification of emperors seems to have been primarily a political device, in the sense that ostracism and the referendum are political devices. Please note that by "device" I do not suggest an exact analogy with the process of mechanical invention, for nothing at all persistent in politics can be as rationally and deliberately devised as a mechanical invention. But I do use the term because its overtones of conscious planning seem to me here to be accurate. Emperor worship provided for a vast and mostly illiterate population of different races, traditions, and beliefs — in short, for an international society — a symbol of the legal unity of the state, a symbol somewhat analogous to the

Crown in the British Commonwealth, or to the Stars and Stripes in our own. Alexander the Great had already made use of emperor worship in an effort to hold together his own hastily assembled aggregation of Greeks and Orientals. The Romans simply took over this device, some of them undoubtedly with their tongues in their cheeks, others with that half-belief many of us moderns have in our own political divinities — such as the Supreme Court of the United States.

The administration of this international state was in the hands of a bureaucracy, or civil service, supplemented in the frontier areas by the military, who in Rome as in the modern world were not entirely unlike the civilian bureaucrats in their disposition and habits. Though high policy, and the drama of history, were made by the emperors and their immediate circles, the undramatic work of holding the state together was done by these administrators, military and civilian. They were in fact responsible only to the Emperor through a central bureaucracy: the Senate was in no important sense a "representative" body, and certainly not representative of the whole Empire. The Empire indeed lacked what we nowadays call a legislative body. We do not as a matter of fact know much in detail about the education of the men who ran this Empire, their social origins, the way in which they were recruited — all the things that as retrospective sociologists we should like to know. But we do know that at the height of the Empire they were widely representative of the various peoples of the Empire, including notably the Greeks. They did not compose an alien, purely Roman group administering the affairs of subject peoples, like the British civil service in India in the nineteenth century. They gradually extended over the Empire the application of a single system of law — a growing and in its best days a flexible system of law. They seem not to have interfered unduly with local customs and peculiarities — indeed Christian tradition has long blamed Pontius Pilate, in some ways a quite typical Roman administrator, for not interfering enough. Whatever the sins of the first generations of Roman exploiters of the provinces — sins familiar to those of us who in the unreformed high schools waded through our Cicero — their successors in Antonine days were by no means mere agents of economic exploitation. In brief, these administrators did an unheroic and imperfect, but as this world goes substantially successful job of running a vast territorial state, and quite without benefit of radio, telegraph, telephone, typewriter, and — essential of all bureaucracies today, business, educational, or governmental — mimeograph machines.

But more important than the actual administrative work of these administrators was the fact that they, together with writers, teachers, philosophers, and

other people we like to call intellectuals, and a certain
number of men of independent incomes, country
gentlemen, big-business men, and the like, made up a
group that can fairly be called a cosmopolitan, or better yet international, elite.[1] Pallas, Narcissus, Seneca,
Epictetus, Plutarch, Herodes Atticus, Ausonius, Rutilius — we know the names, and some of the works, of
many of them, and inevitably we know most about
the intellectuals. But we probably do not have the
sources to study in this elite the kind of questions the
modern sociologist likes to ask about contemporary
elites. We cannot tell just how numerous they were in
proportion to the general population, nor how far they
were refreshed in personnel by the "career open to
talents," nor how great were their authority and prestige, nor what were habits, prejudices, their unintellectual lives, in short. I cannot claim to be an authority

[1] Of course I do not like the word "elite." My Pomona audi-
ence did not like it. It has already become an academic smear-
word, and to be an "elitist" thinker, like Pareto, is to be labeled
a hopeless reactionary, a fascist or worse. But in our democratic
society *all* words or phrases indicating the existence in this society of privileged groups are suspect and subject to cheapening.
(It must have been already noted that in medieval society the
process was exactly the opposite: words describing underpriv-
ileged groups, churl, villain, and the like, originally descriptive,
acquired unfavorable emotional overtones.) If the reader is offended by "elite," I give him the choice of "ruling classes,"
"privileged classes," "upper classes," "aristocracy," or even
"leaders," "bosses," or "big-shots." But I suspect he will be
offended by them all.

on Ancient History, and I have certainly come nowhere near exhausting the bibliography of the subject.
It is quite possible that historians have answered some
of these questions, though in general, and for later
periods with more abundant source materials, they
have not usually undertaken the kind of researches the
sociologists would like them to undertake.

We do, however, know enough about these people to
be able to say quite definitely that they do not seem to
be Greeks, Italians, Iberians, Gauls, Syrians, nor even
in the usual sense Romans, but rather people who have
managed to transcend nationality, who are "citizens
of the world." I suggest that you will see what I mean
if you will think of the most internationally minded
workers for one world in modern times — Wilson, Bri-
and, Streseman, Roosevelt, Willkie, even the dogmatic
pacifists and the crank pamphleteers. Surely they all
have upon them the stamp of their nationalities? And
naturally, for the one world which molded the elite of
the Roman Empire does not exist to mold any of us
today. I hasten to add that I do not mean here anything so silly as that since we have not got a genuine
international state we cannot ever hope to build one
up. I mean merely that the process of building up such
a society was in the ancient world a slow one; and
that when once it had been built it tended to perpet-
uate itself by those processes of education and, in
Bagehot's happy phrase, "unconscious imitation" by

which all societies hold together. We cannot yet have the full advantages of the working of such processes, for we have as yet only the beginnings of an international society within which they can work.

Many of the members of this elite were, of course, bilingual as to Latin and Greek, though there was a rough division of the Empire into a Latin-speaking western half and a Greek-speaking eastern half. The other tongues were hardly recognized as tongues of culture, and it may be said that *culturally* this whole agglomeration was rather a Graeco-Latin diarchy than a genuinely international civilization. Even in this field, however, it should be noted that the intellectuals of the time were by no means unaware of their debt to the ancient civilizations of the Nile and Euphrates valleys and the Orient generally. They had not our modern anthropological interests in the primitive peoples around them, though again one must not exaggerate. Tacitus may have studied the Germans rather as a way of criticizing his fellow countrymen, but he does seem to have studied them with some degree of detachment.

The simpler forms of national self-esteem, such as the racialism we are now so familiar with, were quite impossible for this elite; they were obviously not a race. Moreover, they held, as something rather more than a philosophy if less than a religion, a set of beliefs which provides one of the most consistent bases for a cosmopolitan society ever worked out. This is the Stoic faith, which had among these people in Antonine days the kind of universality the Protestant faith had among Victorian Englishmen. Stoicism went at least as far as did eighteenth-century political thought in declaring for the equality of all mankind. Thomas Paine could hardly have gone beyond Cicero's assertion that "no one thing is as like to another as we [human beings] are like one another."

It is not, however, with the formal doctrines of Stoicism as a system of thought that we should here concern ourselves, but rather with Stoicism as a way of life, as the conditioning of an international elite, as — if you will forgive a rather vulgar anachronism — the "old school tie" of the ancient world. For the purposes of studying the whole behavior of a group of people, their conditioned responses, their automatic behavior, their prejudices, their unthinking as well as their thinking existence, the literary fragments we have left from this period are quite hopelessly inadequate. Nevertheless, one can get some notions of all this from what we know of a man like Plutarch.

Plutarch was no philosopher, and when one calls him a Stoic it is in the rough sense just outlined. He was not even very intelligent, in the sense of constructive analytical intelligence, the kind that Thucydides and Polybius had. He was a literate country gentleman, with encyclopedic interests, and a great fondness

for moralizing. Most of his life was spent in his native
Boeotia, and he seems to have been a good citizen of
Chaeronea as well as a good citizen of the world. His
best-known work, the *Parallel Lives,* would seem to
give him constant occasion to contrast and compare
Romanness with Greekness, and yet that is just what,
in general, he does not do. A Greek, and writing in
Greek, he seems to take Rome and its history as one of
the facts of life. You cannot think of him as either a
Romanophobe or a Romanophile. What I am getting
at will perhaps become clear if I take another modern
instance. The most enlightened modern Englishman
writing about Frenchmen, or the most enlightened
Frenchman writing about Englishmen will show that
he cannot quite take nationalism in stride, will betray
a self-consciousness about being fair and objective.
Or better yet contrast with Plutarch Polybius, who
lived before the Romans had conquered the world, and
who is as aware of the differences between Romans
and Greeks — though in many ways he admires the
Romans — as a Yankee like Emerson is aware of the
differences between Englishmen and Americans.

Plutarch's code seems to have made him, or helped
him become, kindly, upright, dutiful, and, within the
limitations of the Graeco-Roman world, genuinely cosmopolitan in outlook. It will not do, of course, to take
him as a satisfactory sample of a whole class. One
suspects that the responsible administrators were a bit

less idealistic and a bit less credulous than Plutarch. Yet, especially as time goes on, and men born and raised in the once Wild West of the Empire, in Iberia, in Gaul, even in Britain, come into positions of prominence in this elite, it is clear that what I have called the international quality of thinking and feeling of the group continues, and is perhaps even broadened in its scope.

We should not exaggerate the completeness of the adaptation this class had made to its task of holding together such an aggregation of peoples. I have already pointed out that the cultural synthesis they effected was limited essentially to Greek and Roman elements. As Stoics, they tended rather to resist the religious currents that began to flow in from the Orient. For the rest, their culture — and I wish to use culture in a very broad sense to include those elements of non-intellectual conditioning, of habit and tradition I have mentioned before — their culture must seem too excessively authoritarian and imitative, lacking in imagination and enterprise, and totally, or nearly so, without that spur to continual experimental change which modern science has made second nature even to those delicate souls among us who resent the prestige of science and scientists in the modern world. This international society was not a creative society. The best of art, thought, and even of science to come from the ancient world came before the Roman Empire reached its height. And, finally, this elite seems almost isolated from the masses, or at any rate to have less in common with the masses than ruling classes have usually had in Western society.

IV

I have already complained too much, no doubt, over the relative inadequacy of our sources. Yet I must complain once more that I do not see how we can answer properly the very important question as to how the millions of ordinary human beings, slaves, free artisans, peasants, small traders and the like, who came under the rule of this international state really felt toward it. Was a Belgic peasant or a Syrian shopkeeper stirred by a sense of membership in a common thing when he saw the eagles of a legion carried by? Was he perhaps stirred to hatred against outsiders, exploiters? What could the distant Caesar, divine though he was, mean to the provincial who went through the ritual motions of emperor worship? The record of slave revolts and other civil disorders throughout this period shows that what we call the class struggle was a very real thing. How was this class struggle related to any political and territorial loyalties individuals may have felt? Unhappily for us if not for them, there were in those days not only no Gallup polls, but no Letters to the Editor.

Nevertheless I shall hazard as a hunch or first ap-

proximation the statement that in the sense that the
masses clearly feel loyalty to and a sharing in the
modern nation-state (and this in spite of the class
struggle) the masses in the Roman Empire did not
feel loyalty to and a sharing in that state. Or, if you
think that comparison between a multi-national state
like the Roman Empire and our modern unified nation-states is unfair, I shall say that, in the sense that
the masses of the British Commonwealth of Nations
(*not* the dependent British Empire, but the self-governing Dominions) feel loyalty to the Crown, the
masses of the Roman Empire probably did not feel
loyalty to the Emperor. I make this statement very
tentatively, and on the basis of lack of positive evidence and — a proceeding no doubt dangerous for a
historian — on some general ideas about human nature and human behavior. Frankly, I can see no way
in which these masses could have taken part in the
common thing, could have gone through any signifi-
cant actions which made them really aware of such
partaking. And, of course, save for hopeless intellectuals, some form of action is necessary to men before
they can begin to believe, let alone share. It may be
that emperor worship was sufficient, but I doubt it. It
may be that there were some equivalents of the Mar-
seillaise and the Star-Spangled Banner, of the pledge
of allegiance to the flag, of the Fourth of July, of the
Union Jack and the *Life of Nelson,* of the Prussian

cadet schools, of the Lincoln Memorial and all of the rest of the very complex set of ritual and memorial actions by which modern states emotionally symbolize their unity. Some of this there must have been, but it seems to have been stronger toward local than toward imperial things. Even the sentiments of the military, always very strong and, if you will forgive what is not a tautology, very sentimental, seem to have been focused more strongly on the individual legion than in any modern army on the regiment.

Now it seems likely that in any imperial or federal state there must be a kind of balance between the parts and the whole, between local autonomy and centralized control. The Romans from the very beginning of their expansion showed that they did not wish to "Romanize" conquered peoples hastily either by force or by propaganda. There is no close parallel to the process which, during the heyday of nineteenth-century national aggressions, was called "Prussification," "Italianization," "Russification." Indeed it is quite possible that in some ways the Romans were too tolerant; they certainly left to the constituent parts of their empire a very high degree of local and cultural autonomy. There are few good signs that for the great majority of the masses of the Empire anything like imperial patriotism came to supplant, or to transcend, the loyalties of men to tribe, city-state, to the little homeland of immediate experience. Not even the extension under Caracalla of full citizenship to all free men of the Empire seems to have been sufficient to build up for this international state a place in the hearts of its masses. The cults of Mithra and of Isis, the growing faith in Christ — these did indeed show that the sentiments of many men, even of humble and illiterate men, could be moved by universal beliefs far transcending tribe and city-state. But that is a different story.

We need not here rake over the embers of old disputes. We need not even put the question as to how far Christianity was one of the causes of the breakup of the Roman Empire. We must, however, note that in the early centuries of its growth, which coincide with the best years of the Empire, Christianity was at least a non-political, if not an anti-political, way of life. I think we can all agree that by and large the early Christians were not actively interested in preserving and strengthening the sentiments that held men together in the Empire as a common thing. Some of you, I am sure, regard the foregoing statement as a rather extreme example of New England understatement. The wilder extremists among Christians — and they were very conspicuous in the first few centuries of our era — fled the world for desert hermitages, awaited in daily expectancy the destruction of this world, scorned so mundane an occupation as politics. The bulk of Christians even in those times were humble and ordinary people, mostly what we should call proletarians, with a mixture of intellectuals tired and frustrated by the conventions of pagan Stoicism. I cannot say with any confidence that their Christianity made them bad Roman citizens. I must say merely that to the extent that they took seriously the other-worldliness of their religion, to the extent they really believed this world to be the devil's work, they must have failed to make that identification of the self with the political common thing which *must* be made if a state is to have stability. The point is this: we do not know whether Christianity was psychologically inconsistent with the establishment and maintenance of a basis of mass patriotism in the Roman Empire, and we might as well confess that we do not know. We do, however, know pretty surely that no such mass patriotism ever grew up.

Nor is it permissible to risk the generalization that the lack of such mass patriotism was in itself one of the important factors in the fall of this great international state. Into this old question of the fall of the Roman Empire, which has probably been disputed for a longer time than any historical question, I shall not have the temerity to go. I think it worth noting that, in spite of the survival of the Roman *imperium* as something like an obsession in the Middle Ages, and in spite of its revival as something less dignified than an obsession in the days of Mussolini, the real Roman Empire, the international society we have been focusing on for this lecture, had as a going concern a fairly short life, not over two or three centuries. It persisted, and has persisted to this day, but rather as an abstraction, a symbol, an idea, than as a fact, as something of flesh and blood; and where, in the Roman Catholic Church, the Roman *imperium* has survived in flesh and blood, it is in a shape altered, transmuted by its priestly character, by its sometimes reluctant, but nonetheless real acceptance of the separation between lay and spiritual. As a going concern, as a concrete association among men on earth, the Roman international state clearly did not exhibit the kind of recuperative power, the ability to keep itself alive even though it loses its "independence" or "sovereignty," shown in modern times by such oppressed national units as Ireland and Poland.

I know that some of you will disagree with me here. Those of you — and in any representative American company even in these hard-boiled times there will be many of you — who hold that the spirit is more important than the deed, the symbol more important than the fact, will feel that the survival *in idea* of the brief Roman transcendence of nationality, parochialism, particularism, is one of the things that makes it possible for men to organize and consider ways of achieving a new transcendence of nationalism. Nor would I wish by any means to deny this altogether. We *are* helped to think of and to work for international peace and a better association of nations precisely because there was once a Roman *imperium,* just as we are helped to the same end by the fact that there was once a Socrates, a Christ, a Buddha.

But I am at the moment more interested in pointing out how hard in fact it has proved to realize here on earth and in concrete political institutions these noble ideals of peace and good will. The most extensive international state we of Western society have succeeded in building had after all a brief existence as a going concern. It gave effective realization to some of the aspirations of men toward peace for hardly more than Gibbon's dream period of the Antonines. It never solved its very serious economic and social problems; it was never without actual or threatening internal class troubles. It could not, finally, defend itself against decay from within and from barbarian pressure from without.

V

In conclusion, I should like to sum up briefly some elements in the Roman Empire which seem to be important factors in its achievements as an international society — for though impermanent and incomplete, the Empire was such an international society. I do not, of course, mean that we shall thereby get a final formula for building such a society in our own day. I trust

I have already made clear that I have no such blind faith in the possibilities of the study of history. I mean merely to summarize in broad terms a process which I take to be not wholly different from contemporary processes which interest us very much.

First, the Empire was a real state, with an administrative hierarchy and a legal system which had authority throughout its territories; and it had in the institution of emperor worship and in the very extensive (finally universal) Roman citizenship at least the rudiments of a system of symbols by which individual citizens were given concrete evidence of what they shared as Romans. Second, the constituent parts of the Empire were not forced into any common mold, cultural or, as far as local affairs went, political; on the contrary, the Empire was a congeries of races, languages, religions, ways of life, so that the common man in most parts of the Empire was hardly touched in his daily life by the fact of his membership in a universal state. Third, this congeries seems to have been held together largely by a numerically small elite, some of whom carried on the actual administration of the state. This elite seems to have been genuinely loyal to the Empire as an international state, to have worked well for it, to have had almost no signs of what we call today "national prejudices," in short, to have been a genuinely cosmopolitan ruling class. Their system of beliefs, which can be adequately summed up as a not too philosophical Stoicism, seems to have been admirably suited to be the faith of such a cosmopolitan ruling class. Their habits, their conditioning, again suggest that they were well trained for their task. Fourth, there seems to have been no great popular participation in this international society and state. The masses, illiterate and depressed, many of them in slavery, seem remote from their well-intentioned Stoic leaders. The Roman Empire was never a state of the people.

Yet, in spite of its weaknesses and cruelties and failures, and in spite of its brief life of effectiveness, so brief in comparison with the permanence of Egypt or China, the Roman Empire has left in the minds of us Westerners a memory on which to anchor our deep desire for some kind of unity, for some solution of the problem of organized warfare, for peace on earth. An immense literature echoes the tribute of Rutilius, has echoed it so long that the line has become a tag for occasions like this: *urbem fecisti quod prius orbis erat.*

A MEDIEVAL AND A MODERN INSTANCE

II

A MEDIEVAL AND A MODERN INSTANCE

We are often told by admirers of the Middle Ages that in fact there was in the thirteenth century a unity among Western men at least as firm as that of Antonine Rome. I am very anxious to avoid debate here as to the reality of the much-discussed medieval unity. I think it clear that there survived in the minds of educated men some notion of the one world of the Romans, that for these same men the unity of Christendom was a necessity of faith, that Latin was a genuinely international tongue, that among nobles the forms of chivalry transcended nationality as well as common sense. Nevertheless, it remains true even at the height of medieval civilization, that the practice of local and private war persisted, that the actual effective governing of men was subject to an extreme subdivision of power, that, in short, the Europe of the Middle Ages was divided into hundreds, indeed thousands, of political units independent enough to make war among themselves. Medieval Europe was in its international relations a world of extreme disintegration.

It is the process by which a greater unit, France, was in the course of centuries built up from hundreds of feudal units that I wish to consider now. About 1100 A.D., for instance, it was sweet and fitting for a man from Normandy to die and kill for his duke, and for a man from Paris to die and kill for his king. Subinfeudation may have confused many good men in this matter of ultimate loyalties, but they all thought the ultimate loyalty could somehow be found on earth. Within a few centuries, Normandy became, as we say coldly in the textbooks, a part of France; Normans became Frenchmen, and no longer legally killed Frenchmen. What is true of Normandy eventually became true of Brittany, Flanders, Languedoc, Dauphiné, and all the rest of what now seems to some of us *la France éternelle*.

Here, perhaps, we had best dodge one of the great insoluble problems of human history. France has been, especially since 1789, so nearly the complete nation-state, so nearly unified in culture and habits, disunited only in the half-unreal struggle of party politics, that we are likely to regard her building-up from these medieval fragments as somehow predetermined, "natural," and therefore inevitable. It seems impossible that France could ever have been other than she is. And, at the same time, we may tell ourselves pessimistically that to go beyond the nation-state, to build something new and greater from units like France, is unnatural, artificial, and therefore impossible. You can see what opportunities for metaphysical debate yawn in front of us. I shall not attempt to settle the question of historical determinism. It will be enough if I say that it seems to me that the creation of France from hundreds of warring units is a process in which human will, human motives, human strength and weakness all had a part, and that we as human beings can in some senses learn from what these other human beings did and suffered.

II

One thing is especially clear. The French state, like the Roman state, was built up around a very strong symbol of power and unity. Perhaps never, even in the extreme disintegration of the Dark Ages, was the notion of a symbolic "sovereignty" embodied in some real person altogether absent in the kingdom of France. But clearly, with the growth of the power of the Capetian kings after the tenth century, the unifying strength of the French Crown had become very great indeed. Though French republican historians have fairly consistently sought to deny or minimize the fact, it is obvious that even as late as 1789 the common people of France felt a very real loyalty to the person of the King. And, of course, the building of France during the long reign of the Capetians owed a great deal to the fact that their administration, their army, their judiciary formed a solid legal core around which the regularities of French daily life could be

ordered. Indeed, since to all but the stubbornest believers in the doctrine that no individual destiny
counts in the impersonal flow of historical forces such
accidents are very important, the successful building
of the French nation-state of today owes something to
the good luck of the Capetians in procreating male
children consistently for hundreds of years.

You will recall that in my first chapter I distinguished for purposes of analysis between political integration by the method of force, or imperialism, and
that by the method of consent, or federalism. The
union of France was on the whole achieved imperialistically. To the cell-unit of the *Ile de France*, the nucleus of modern France, other units were added, in
general, without their own specific consent. Yet force
is a somewhat misleading word to describe a process in
which guile, luck, diplomacy, and even consent are
also present, and in which our old acquaintance, the
the economic factor, is hard at work.

War was, however, one of the ways through which
the *Ile de France* became simply *la France*. Normandy
came in through a war in which the Duke, better
known to us as King John of England, was beaten by
his feudal overlord the King of France. That very important part of the French state known as Languedoc
dropped eventually into the lap of the Capetians
through a war they did not have to wage primarily
themselves. Medieval Languedoc was one of the cen-

ters of a heresy, the Manichaean, very objectionable to the orthodox. With papal encouragement a crusade was preached and carried out, the Manichaeans were put down, and the lands of the Counts of Toulouse, who had not been able to cope with the heresy in addition to the other troubles that beset a feudal lord, were added to the lands of the French kings. Well into modern times, in 1766 in fact, Lorraine finally fell into the French monarchy as the end result of a long course of planning and negotiating which, had I but time to go into it, would give a nice detailed illustration of the complexities of the process by which the one France was built out of many parts. But note that even the acquisition of Lorraine depended at one crucial point on war, the now almost forgotten war of the Polish Succession of 1733–35. As a result of that war, the French-backed but unsuccessful claimant to the throne of Poland, Stanislas Leszczynski, was compensated with the Duchy of Lorraine, vacated by the elevation of the Duke to be consort of the heiress of all the Hapsburgs, Maria Theresa. Stanislas's sole heir, Maria Leszczynska, was successfully if not happily married to Louis XV of France, and at the death of her father Lorraine came at last into the kingdom of France.

The final acquisition of Alsace, achieved roughly a century earlier than that of Lorraine, is an excellent example of another phase of the making of united

France. Here the Capetians were heavily indebted to their civil administrators, and especially to their lawyers. A great deal of Alsace was added to the Crown piecemeal in the seventeenth century under Louis XIV, as a result of the work of the *chambres de réunion,* boards of experts who went systematically over the incredibly complicated nexus of feudal holdings in a given area, and who were sooner or later always able to unearth a parchment which proved that someone either related to or dependent on the royal family of France had held this or that bit of land, or that a town had had a royal charter, or that an abbey was dependent on a French abbey — at any rate, they were always able to prove that the land was a part of France. My teachers were good children of the nineteenth century, and even believed in self-determination of peoples, so I was brought up to regard these *chambres de réunion* as most iniquitous instruments of royal tyranny imposed on virtuous Alsatians. My teachers were also pro-French and anti-German, and felt that Bismarck had been even harsher toward the Alsatians than had Louis XIV. I remember that I concluded from all this that the Alsatians should have been left free and independent, neither French nor German — and that even as far back as that I still had my doubts about how many "free and independent" peoples there was room for in Europe.

Brittany is the best example of a bit of territory

coming in by the simple expedient of marriage, but of course Brittany was peopled with Celts who didn't even speak French, and the successful absorption of Brittany in the spiritual unity of France had to await modern times. There are a few ardent souls who want Brittany to be quite independent, but since even in 1940 the Germans were wholly unable to stir up any effective movement to separate Brittany from France, I think we can say that here too, whatever the method, we have a successful example of the making of one from many.

Most important of all factors, perhaps, is the growth in France of representative government. This is something new, something the Roman Empire did not have. Here, as so often in this book, we must avoid fascinating subjects for debate. Historians are by no means agreed as to the origins and nature of early representative government in Europe. The old notion that medieval representative bodies are all descended from a completely democratic Germanic tribal assembly has pretty well gone by the board, as has also the notion of an English monopoly of representative government. Most historians would probably agree that in France kings like Philip the Fair used the Estates General (parliament) to further their own centralizing ends against the centrifugal forces of feudalism, and that they had no notion of producing, fortifying, or consulting a French "nation" with a "general will."

Yet in effect the Estates General, the provincial Estates, even such dubiously "representative" bodies as the *parlements*, preserved throughout French history the continuity of representative government. This clearly is a federalistic, rather than an imperialistic, element in making from many one in France. Yet in origin it is almost certainly a piece of royal initiative; it was never "planned" to be what it became, a bridge to popular government. It was not even a "popular" movement.[1]

But there is no use carrying this catalogue further here. One could dwell at length on many other aspects of the building of France — on, for instance, the somewhat restive collaboration between the Crown and the new bourgeois elite of the growing towns. In all these aspects, however, one recurs constantly to the importance of the Crown as a symbol of union, and to the human agents of the Crown as workers for union.

Here, as in the Roman Empire, there is then also an

[1] I confess that I composed these last sentences with my mind on the more extreme of the enthusiasts for world federation, the pathetic youngsters who refuse to work through anyone tainted with government responsibilities, or indeed any kind of responsibilities in the wicked, conventional world. These youngsters expect the parliament of man to come direct from purely private initiative. Of course the "people" do not start, let alone carry through, anything at all, from folk tunes to revolutions. I can think of no examples of the success of the kind of movement favored by those who wish to avoid any governmental action in solving our international problems. The nearest I can come is the Children's Crusade.

elite in the service of the larger unit, an elite first of all French in thought and feeling, and as time goes on, hardly Norman, Flemish, Gascon, Provençal at all, save in the picturesque sense so dear to novelists of local color. As to the formation of that elite there is, I think, a general misunderstanding nurtured by the textbooks, and sprung, like so many other misunderstandings of French history, from the bitter partisanship of the Great Revolution. It is not true to say that the Crown in alliance with the *bourgeoisie* made French unity against the opposition of the feudal nobility; and that once unity was made this nobility was suddenly transformed into a group of fawning courtiers, mere parasites on the nation. The true relation of the French nobility to national unity is far subtler. As great lords, many of these nobles did indeed work for local and particular, certainly selfish ends, and did oppose the centralizing work of the Crown. Yet culturally many of them were French, as contrasted with provincial, long before the end of the Middle Ages. They fought against their sovereign sometimes; but at other times they fought on his side, they went on Crusades with him, and they took part in his councils and helped administer his realm. Their famous code of chivalry, which again represents the kind of conditioned, unintellectual behavior I have previously pointed out among the Stoics, came to be perhaps even more French than feudal. They did, indeed, have a strong sense of caste. Possibly, as Shaw suggests in his *Saint Joan*, a fifteenth-century English nobleman felt nearer to a French nobleman than to an English swineherd. The pride of ancient nobility has lingered on. I am told that English aristocrats of the real old stock rather look down on the present British royal family as *parvenus* — as indeed they are. Yet this does not prevent these aristocrats being patriotic Englishmen. On the whole, I think there is good evidence that European aristocracies have in the past had a large part in the building of their respective nationalities, that is, in the process of political integration.

At any rate, by the close of the Middle Ages there had grown up in France an elite French rather than Norman, Breton, or Gascon, an elite recruited from nobles of the sword, from nobles of the gown, from ennobled bourgeois, and from plain bourgeois. There was already in fact the nucleus of a bureaucracy which was to last until 1789, and in some senses, to this day. Already the businessmen were working for the larger markets of the nation-state. One of these latter, Jacques Coeur of Bourges, has come to stand, like the Fuggers of Germany, as a symbol for the new power of commercial wealth.

Many things bound these people together as a ruling class, though of course as individuals they were usually in intense, indeed sometimes literally in cutthroat, competition among themselves for place and power. They were, on the whole, loyal to the Crown. They spoke that form of North French which had by early modern times emerged as classic French. They already felt themselves part of *France, mère des arts, des armes, et des lois*. They had, save for the brief Calvinist flare-up of the sixteenth century, their religion in common. And note that, though in Germany both in medieval and in early modern times organized Christianity was politically a divisive force, in France Christianity proved for the most part to be a force for union. A figure like St. Louis, the canonized King Louis IX of France, as you see him in the pages of Joinville, suggests that both French Crown and Gallican Church were already by the thirteenth century aware that each had more to gain from collaboration than from quarreling. And yet Louis and his nobles as Joinville pictures them are certainly "medieval" enough in their habits, loyalties, and ideas.

When we come to the masses, we once more run up against the difficulty we encountered in attempting to measure the extent to which the masses in the Roman Empire felt loyalty toward the state. Historians of old simply were not much concerned with the masses, save as a sort of backdrop for the actions of the great. On medieval and early modern France we are, however, well enough informed to know that the majority of ordinary Frenchmen did not speak French. They spoke Breton, Flemish, German, Basque, Provençal, or one of the very numerous dialects of the Languedoc or the Languedoïl which were mutually unintelligible. They cannot possibly have had the cohesiveness, the sense of oneness, the feeling for France as *la patrie,* which has been the product of the intensive education of Frenchmen in nationalism since 1789, an education admirably studied by Carlton Hayes in his *France: A Nation of Patriots.* Indeed, during the world war which broke out in 1792 a law was passed requiring the registration of foreigners (*étrangers*) in each town or village. Many of these registers of foreigners contain names unmistakably French; the local authorities had simply registered as foreigners anyone not of the locality.[2] I have been a summer resident of Vermont for twenty years, and am of course still essentially a foreigner in Vermont; but I do not think the town clerk would ever go so far as to *register* me as a foreigner.

Yet, if the centrifugal forces seem strong in the lives of these masses of the provincial French, there are clearly also strong centripetal forces. I have already pointed out that even in 1789 it was clear that the country people — that is, four out of every five Frenchmen — were loyal to Louis XVI as the symbol

[2] See for this J. B. Sirich, *The Revolutionary Committees in the Departments of France, 1793–1794* (Harvard University Press, 1943), page 21.

of French unity. The Crown of France served something of the same purpose as did emperor worship in the Roman Empire. If the higher clergy as part of the French ruling classes helped forge the unity of France, it is equally true that the lower clergy, the parish priests, were for generations links between the villages and the greater outside world, links to Paris as well as to Rome; indeed, once the Gallican Church was firmly in the saddle early in modern times, links rather to Paris than to Rome.

Finally, it is a commonplace that the unity of France was in part hammered out on the anvil of the Hundred Years' War with England. Joan of Arc certainly did not work with the mass national armies of a later time, when the Revolution had made of France a nation-state in the modern sense. In many respects, her methods and even her aims were medieval. Yet in the long perspective the value of Joan's achievement for the building of a French national patriotism on a broad popular basis was very great indeed. Perhaps because the term has become in our times too much of a formula, I hesitate to say that the myth of Joan is more important than what she did in her brief lifetime. Obviously the myth could never have grown had she not done very great things. It remains true that, as we cannot think of the United States without Lincoln, we cannot think of France without Joan of Arc. A world-state, too, will need its heroes; and, no matter what

debunkers say, you cannot successfully make syn-
thetic heroes. Our best present possibilities — a Kant,
a Tom Paine, a Briand, a Wilson, a Karl Marx, a
Lenin, even a Franklin Roosevelt — seem to me inadequate.

III

I have taken France as an example of the way in
which a great modern nation-state has been built up
— or, if you prefer a figure that suggests an organic
process, has grown up. Had I taken England, the time-
scheme and many of the details would have been
different, but not radically so. After all, what we call
England was at the beginning of the Middle Ages divided into a number of squabbling kingdoms, the Hep-
tarchy of our schoolbooks. Under the House of Wessex
a kind of union had been achieved by the eleventh
century, a union which might or might not have
proved permanent. The Norman Conquest, in the long
run a very lucky thing for England, ensured for the
kingdom a centralized administration which gave England effective national unity rather earlier than any of
her continental rivals.

Had I chosen to take the case of Germany I should
have had to analyze a case very different as to details
and timing, but not in kind, I think, different from
the cases of France and England. Germany too started
with an extreme feudal disintegration, attained after

Charlemagne the rather phony integration repre-
sented by the Holy Roman Empire of the German
People, lay divided for centuries under the contrary
stresses put on her by her great French neighbor and
her own titular leaders, the Hapsburgs, whose lands
and interests were half outside Germany, and only
yesterday, in 1870, achieved through Bismarck's policy of "blood and iron" the status of a nation-state.
The consequences of the Germans' delayed attainment of what every people seems to want, independent
statehood, have been very grave for all of us. A thor-
ough study of Germany as a case history in what I
call the process of political integration would, of
course, be essential in any well-rounded explanation
of how that process has got as far as it has in our
Western society. I have, however, already indicated
that I cannot pretend to achieve here any such completeness, and that I am interested rather in first approximations, in attempting to show, if only in outline
form, the importance of the study of political integration in the past.

We can, however, risk the generalization that not
even the instance of Germany proves what the Nazi
race theorists maintained, that is, that there exists a
mystic, natural, and therefore irresistible force which
determines that the final form of the state in our society shall be the unified, sovereign, nation-state based
on ethnic homogeneity. The example of Switzerland

is perhaps overworked by the few optimists still left in this harsh world, but after all Switzerland does exist, and is not based on any of the identities of language, race, religion, which the theorists of nationalism commonly take as determinants of nation-statehood. Flemings and Walloons quarrel within Belgium, but the sufferings of two wars seem rather to have affirmed than to have weakened the statehood of Belgium. The fact surely is that if "natural" is taken to mean "determined by certain inborn and indelible characteristics of the human organism," the boundaries and the human make-up of none of the states of Europe — not even France, not even Britain — are "natural." All are "artificial," the result of hundreds of years of complex interactions among their peoples, the result, at least in part, of the kind of deliberate human activity I am not afraid of calling by a name some of you may dislike — "planning." Deliberate human volition went into the making of France or Germany. Deliberate human volition, if patient and realistic, ought not to be incapable of carrying political integration beyond the point achieved in the making of France or Germany, or any other contemporary nation-state.

IV

Before I attempt in my last chapter to see in what way a study of the past of political integration can help us to understand present problems of international relations, I should like to have recourse once more to the case method to survey an element in the problem to which we have as yet not given serious attention. I mean the clear-cut failure of a serious and long-continued effort to achieve political integration. Some of you will perhaps have anticipated me when I say that Ireland seems to me a classic instance of such a failure. It is now nearly eight hundred years since the Norman-English Strongbow and his followers crossed from England to Ireland, and only a very optimistic person would say that the Irish question has at last been settled by the successful inclusion of all Irishmen among the willing subjects of George VI. Eight hundred years, I should like to point out, is a very long time, even in Europe. It is rather a striking thing to note that of the Celtic people — if, after my strictures on Nazi theories of race you will forgive my using the label "Celtic" — the Bretons, the Welsh, the Scots, and the Irish, only the last have failed to adapt themselves to some kind of working political union with their French or English neighbors. The Bretons, though many of them still speak only Breton, and though of course there are romantic nationalists among them who say they want independence, are on the whole loyal citizens of the French Republic. The Welsh, who also speak their own language, talk occasionally of Home Rule, or complain that nowadays they haven't even a Prince of Wales, but to an outside observer they seem to be not very restive members of the United Kingdom. The Scots are, in spite of the vogue for kilts, haggis and Bonnie Prince Charlie set by Sir Walter Scott, not in their rich and populous Lowlands really Celtic at all. Lest I offend any MacGregors or Mackintoshes among you, I hasten to add that the Highlanders are indeed Celts, and that they have flavored the whole of Scotland and of Scottish history. But the important point is that, though just as one hears of Home Rule for Wales so one hears of Home Rule for Scotland, the union of Scotland and England in Great Britain has been, and continues to be, one of the successful instances of political integration.

The union of Ireland with Great Britain was certainly not a success, and in our own day has for twenty-six of the thirty-two counties of Ireland been so nearly dissolved by the creation of Eire as to be almost complete separation. Tenuous legal threads do indeed bind Mr. De Valera's Eire to the greater unity of the lands which owe allegiance to George VI, or at least use his consular services abroad. But we are not here concerned with the puzzling question as to the juridical status of the twenty-six counties. Nor can we, instructive though it might be, study the ways in which the Bretons and the Welsh have reconciled themselves to political integration with the French and the English. I propose to limit myself to a brief study of what I shall call the English-Scottish-Irish triangular relationship, or more specifically, to ask why the English-Scottish relationship has on the whole been a success, and the English-Irish relationship on the whole a failure.

Race theories have here supplied a final explanation that satisfied many, especially those of English stock: the Irish, so this explanation runs, are by decree of nature making them Irish rendered incapable of conducting the business of government at all efficiently. They are volatile, charming, and quite impractical. I have an English friend who maintains that wherever you find in history the name of an Irishman who has amounted to something in politics, literature, science, or business, you will find that he is no pure Celt, but has some good sound Anglo-Saxon chromosomes in his make-up. I shall not attempt here to controvert at length such simple theories. They clearly do not solve our problem, which is why the Irish Celts had a fate so different from that of the Breton, Welsh, and Highland Celts. If there is some biological inheritance that makes all Celts politically at once incompetent to rule themselves and unable to accept the rule of their betters then the histories of Brittany, Wales, and Highland Scotland should be like the history of Ireland, which they are not. Moreover, as an adopted Bostonian, I am reluctant to admit as a fact the assertion that the Irish are unable to run anything

since they certainly run Boston and, contrary to outside liberal belief, have not run it into the ground.

The really important point for us to note is that
over the centuries Scotsmen have gradually come to
feel that what they want as Scots is not incompatible
with their membership in the United Kingdom; and
the Irish have not come to feel that what they want
as Irishmen is compatible with such membership. It
goes without saying to a modern reader that economics has something to do with the matter. On the
whole, Scotsmen have not been exploited economically
by the English. Union with England helped rather
than hindered the growth of the industrial revolution
in the Lowlands. England and the Empire opened a
career to ambitious Scots, and though the notion that
Scots really run the Empire is a stereotype of the
music halls and not a truth, still there can be no doubt
that the union opened a wide field to Scottish initiative
in business and administration. In Ireland, the union
which finally came in 1801 meant no more than continued exploitation of Irish peasants by absentee land-
lords, English or Anglicized, and could not undo the
long years during which the growth of industry in
most of Ireland had been deliberately prevented by
the ruling class in England.

Nor can the importance of religious differences be
neglected. That Roman Catholic countries are not
necessarily industrially backward is amply proven by

Belgium and the Rhineland. Ireland did not stay poor and inefficient because she remained Catholic, any more than Scotland became comparatively rich because she accepted Calvinism. At any rate, no neat positive correlation between Protestantism and Prosperity is possible. What is important is that after the Elizabethan and Cromwellian experiences, in all Ireland, save for those parts of Ulster in which Calvinist Scots were settled by methods highly familiar to us in these days of displaced persons and forcible removals, the Roman Catholic religion came to be synonymous with being Irish. Organized Christianity, though in ideal and in principle it transcends nationality, has on occasion been one of the most potent forces behind nationalism, and nowhere more so than in southern Ireland. When in the late seventeenth and early eighteenth centuries the English attempted through the penal laws to proscribe the public profession of the Roman Catholic religion in Ireland, the alliance between the Irish people and the Church was sealed more strongly than ever.

The penal code was passed in fright by a minority, the English of the "garrison" and their adherents, after the Irish rising in behalf of James II. The intent of these laws can hardly have been to convert the Irish Catholics; on the other hand, they stopped well short of the kind of frightfulness we have come to know in Nazi policy toward the Jews. They merely deprived the Catholics of any civil life, and indeed, of any civil rights. A good dramatic instance is the law that forbade a Catholic to own a horse worth more than five pounds. Any Protestant by giving him this amount could in law force his Catholic neighbor to surrender to him any horse he might have. I think it pretty certain that much of the penal code was never really enforced; but that it should exist at all was an unbearable wound for the Irish.

The penal laws were, then, a complete failure — or rather, they did the opposite of what one assumes their framers intended. They strengthened the mass of the Irish in their Irishness, in their devotion to the Catholic faith, in their hostility to the English and the Anglicized Irish — in short, they finished the work of centuries and made the effective political integration of Irish and English impossible for generations to come.

You will perhaps have noted that I have been constantly talking in terms of the way Irishmen thought, felt, believed. This I have done deliberately. Whatever the complex historical process, with its economic, institutional, military, and intellectual phases, which dug the gulf between England and Ireland, by modern times that gulf had become a psychological gulf. Irishmen had come to hate Englishmen, to feel that the political relations between England and Ireland were such as to hurt Irishmen in ways vital to their existence. They wanted to be, as Irishmen, free from English rule. They were quite obviously under an English rule which had been imposed upon them in part, at least, because they had been beaten by the English in war, and because some of their number had gone over to the English side. They were underdogs, and they could not hide from themselves that they were underdogs.

The Irish had, in short, become obsessive nationalists, and their nationalism was clearly colored by their sense of inferiority. I hope that I am fully aware of the weaknesses and inadequacies of the science of psychology as an instrument for the study of the behavior of the individual; and I am certainly aware of the dangers of treating groups, such as a nation, as though they were individual personalities. I apply terms like "obsession" and "sense of inferiority" to the behavior of the Irish people in full awareness of the vagueness and inaccuracy of the terms; I have known many individual Irishmen to whom such terms in no sense apply. Yet I still think they will do as first approximations, as working generalizations. Needless to say, and I hope those who are of Irish extraction will take this to heart, I am trying to use these terms without overtones of dispraise. I am trying to diagnose, not to condone or to condemn.

What I mean may come out concretely if I cite a speech I heard made many years ago in the Oxford

Union by a brilliant Irishman, who, though he was studying at Oxford, had by no means gone over to the English. After a comparatively brief review of his countrymen's past and present grievances — this was in the days of the black-and-tans — he came to the conclusion that what the Irishman needed was something definite, measurable, even a little vulgar and utilitarian in the way of a collective Irish achievement in which he could take pride. Had he such an achievement, he need not take consolation in things hard to measure, such as Irish soulfulness, Irish depth, Irish romance, Irish nearness to God. One good thumping military victory by the Irish over the British would, he thought, have made a big difference. "If only," he sighed, "we'd had a Bannockburn!" They had, instead, Boyne Water and Vinegar Hill.

Yet of recent years Irish collective self-esteem has been immensely heightened by the success of the revolution which began in 1916. The Irish have won their freedom from the English, in spite of the great economic and military superiority of the United Kingdom. The six counties of Ulster remain as a kind of *Eire irredenta,* and while they so remain, one can hardly conclude that the Irish question is solved. Yet it is more nearly solved than seemed possible a generation ago, and, if I may anticipate some of the things I shall say in my last chapter, solved to the extent that the English-Irish relation has approached the federal relation of government by mutual concession and consent.

What I have said about Ireland could, with a few concrete changes, also be said about Poland. The Polish state for nearly a hundred and fifty years ceased to exist on the map; but it never ceased to exist in the minds and hearts of millions of Poles. To some of the kind of people who like to call themselves "realists," this persistence of oppressed nationalities like the Irish and the Poles is, I suspect, rather annoying. They can hardly deny the fact of such persistence, but on their own principles they can hardly explain it. The conquerors had the power: why didn't they use it to crush the conquered? The conquered really wanted to live as well as possible: why didn't they accept assimilation with their successful enemies, who must by simple evolutionary standards have been more fit than they?

The answers, for those not afflicted with realism, are clear enough. The human sentiments that bind men into nationalities are deep, slow to change, and like many other human sentiments, are often strengthened by attempts to suppress them. As for the conquerors, they too are human. They have not commonly displayed the constant determination, the ruthlessness, the ability to avoid laziness and sloppiness, which would be necessary if they were to exterminate the conquered, or by continued oppression break their national will. It remains a fact that extremely few nationalities, extremely few self-conscious territorial, religious, or even cultural groups have been actually wiped out, destroyed, in our modern Western society. We may find a way to induce nationalities to get along with one another without recourse to war; we shall hardly, if the past is any guide at all, find a way to destroy within any brief period nationalities and the persistent human sentiments that go to make nationalism.

I do not contend that nationalism is unchanging, eternal, but merely that it is extraordinarily persistent and slow to change. The Icelanders, after years of purely nominal dependence on Denmark, have only the other day declared their complete independence. In Spain, Catalonian separatism remains a threat to any central Spanish government. The little Central American republics, after experimenting with, or perhaps merely flirting with, federation, returned to their precarious sovereignty. It is true that the "nation" Mr. Gladstone declared that Jefferson Davis had made in 1861 did not endure. Our Southern fellow citizens seem still on occasion to display some of those traits of obsessive preoccupation with the wrongs inflicted on them by Yankees that characterize oppressed nationalities like the Irish and the Poles. Even Mr. Arnall of Georgia, who is by no means an unreconstructed Southerner, seems to hate Boston as unreasonably as Irishmen used to hate London. But on the whole the South has been assimilated. A distinguished Spaniard visiting this country is said to have remarked that he couldn't understand why the Southerners didn't try it again; his own countrymen would certainly have kept on attempting to revolt! Perhaps Southern nationalism did not have quite enough tradition, quite enough centuries, behind it; perhaps, after 1876 and the abandonment of Reconstruction, the South won the war after all. At any rate, the South has been no Ireland.

Any successful political integration must, then, leave no festering sores of unsatisfied nationalism, no *irredenta,* internal or external. In theory, of course, you might have successful *territorial* integration, at least, if the people of unit A simply exterminated all the inhabitants of unit B. I have, however, already indicated that — again to judge from the historical record — enough human beings have never been consistently inhuman long enough to achieve such an end. Not even we Americans have succeeded in exterminating the Red Indians. Some tribes were indeed annihilated, but at present there are still at least half as many Indians within the United States as there were in 1492; and they are increasing steadily in numbers. I need not point out that the Nazis were not wholly successful in any of their attempts at what is barbarously called — and it is a barbarous thing — genocide.

We must, then, find some way to satisfy the sentiments of nationalism and yet see to it that those sentiments do not express themselves in war. We cannot eradicate these sentiments, or their equivalents, for they are something like a constant of human nature. Years ago, when I was younger and much more hopeful, I ran across a phrase of the English writer Clutton-Brock, in which he defines nationalism as "pooled self-esteem." The phrase impressed me greatly at the time. It coincided with my own superior internationalist scorn for the narrow selfishness that had got us all involved in the current World War of 1914. I inclined then to the belief that if everybody could only see that patriotism is merely pooled self-esteem, they would repudiate so ungenerous a sentiment, and become good citizens of the world.

I now think that to define nationalism as pooled self-esteem is to define it as something enduringly human. For though the forms and means by which people nourish their self-esteem change, though, to borrow again from the commonplaces of psychology, self-esteem can be sublimated into very noble actions, there remains among us poor creatures a sense of personal integrity which no amount of ethical name-changing can really greatly alter. We all have to have grounds for self-esteem. One of those grounds is being Irish, and therefore being somehow a better achievement than a mere Englishman. One of those grounds is being American, and therefore being more up-to-date, more civilized, more hygienic, more progressive, more energetic, more of everything good than any member of backward nationalities like the French, the Italian, the British. I have known G. I.'s from American urban or rural slums holding forth in British pubs on the regrettable material, and especially sanitary, primitiveness of British middle-class life.

But I need hardly pursue this subject further. We have learned from the experience of Rome and of France that the process of political integration, though usually a slow one, is one that has in the past proved to be within the limits of human possibilities. And we have learned from the example of Ireland that if in an attempt at political integration any considerable group of human beings feels that it is being put upon, oppressed, prevented from being what God and Nature intended it to be, the attempt will not succeed. It is no piece of sentimentalism to declare that in the long run all government rests on the consent, or at least on the habits, of the governed. This is merely an obvious induction from the experience of our Western society.

Any effective plan for an international society must, then, take into account existing national loyalties. I say "take into account," not "be abandoned because of." Though the confirmed idealist will not admit it, successful reform is usually based, not on making men have nobler sentiments, but on re-directing, re-focusing, their existing sentiments, on activating some of their sentiments, and on quieting others. We should not aim to make Americans simply sink their love of America in a superior love for all humanity. At the beginning of the great development of modern science, Francis Bacon urged men to turn aside from impossible searches, such as that for the philosopher's stone, and turn their attention to the modest and neglected possibilities of manipulating their actual environment. As a guide for them, he urged the famous aphorism *natura non vincitur nisi parendo* — "nature is not to be commanded save by obeying her." I suggest that in the social sciences we should turn the aphorism to our own use, saying merely that *human* nature is not to be commanded save by obeying her.

It is true that one very human part of human nature is the disposition to believe that a new law, a new constitution, the single tax, the world-state, any product of man's gift for building in Cloud-Cuckoo-Land, will pull us through to better things if only we can set it up in statute book or treaty. I admit that the problem of using productively this sort of human energy, the energy of the simple-minded idealist in a hurry, seems to me almost insoluble. But usually there are not very many such people, and they rarely attain positions of responsibility. Ordinary human nature, which is not idealistic, is perhaps easier to cope with, if one is not in too much of a hurry. We can, I hope, someday pool our self-esteem in something bigger than the nation-state. Surely it is not always later than we think?

THE CONTEMPORARY PROBLEM

III

THE CONTEMPORARY PROBLEM

Before I take on, modestly I hope, the role of prophet I should like to review summarily and very broadly what can be quite solidly established as the experience of the past in the maintenance of peace by political integration.

First of all, it is certain that we of Western society have never, in our five thousand years of recorded history, kept peace for long within an area save by bringing that area within the authority of a single government. Leagues, alliances, ententes, the subtlest or the simplest forms of balance of power, the Truce of God, the Peace of God — by none of these have men kept peace for more than a generation. That generalization is as certain an induction from history as I know. In short, those proponents of a world-state who maintain that long-lasting peace is impossible among sovereign states would seem to be right.

Second, the authority of a single government has, in the past, been extended territorially in a variety of ways, which for purposes of analysis can be sorted into a polarity of force and consent, of imperialism and federalism. The federal solution has been far less common than the imperialist solution in the initial

steps of political integration, but successfully integrated states have almost always proved in practice
to rest on a mixture of force and consent, of imperialism and federalism.

Third, once the newly integrated state has become
a going concern, it is possible to distinguish certain
general characteristics which seem to be necessary
characteristics of any international or supranational
state in our own time. These general characteristics,
these uniformities are: a) a symbolic head of state,
in the past of our Western society almost always an
individual, but an individual made symbol by cere-
monial pomp, ritual, etiquette, and if you like, by
"propaganda"; b) an elite, not always an aristocracy
in the conventional European sense of the word, an
elite commonly charged with responsibility for administration, for setting the tone of society and education,
conditioned morally as well as intellectually to the
service of the integrated state, thoroughly cosmopolitan or international in outlook; c) at least some
loyalty on the part of the masses who live under its
authority, though this loyalty would seem both more
widespread and deeper in such examples of integration
as the modern nation-state than it was in the really
international Roman Empire; d) some degree of local
autonomy, especially where there is among the constituent units a tradition of self-rule; e) an absence
of groups, and especially of groups with a territorial

basis, which feel that the existence of the integrated state is incompatible with their own existence. This last point is merely the negative aspect of the previous one about autonomy, and comes down in practice to this: no integrated political unit can afford to have its Irelands, its Polands, its *irredenta*.

Finally, in the past the process of political integration has almost invariably been a slow one, whether it came about imperialistically or federally. The Roman Empire, the great modern nation-states like France, Britain, Germany took centuries in the making, and no one specific historical act can be taken as in itself wholly a determinant in their making. Here as so often American experience is in a sense unique. Our Constitutional Convention at Philadelphia in 1787 does seem to have made the beginnings of a nation. Yet, just as we nowadays cannot quite think of the Constitution as "struck off by the mind of man" in one moment, so we cannot think historically of the building of the American nation without the preparatory work of the colonial period — and without the great test of the Civil War.

II

There is, then, in the past of our civilization little — indeed, no — precedent for the immediate success of the kind of effort well-meaning men and women are now making in the cause of world government and a sovereign world-state. Were the historian to desert his serious and dignified business and turn bookmaker, he would be obliged to say that the odds against the world federationists are prohibitive, astronomical. But perhaps the historian ought not to be consulted here at all? Perhaps these are *unprecedented* times in fact as so often in our rhetoric; perhaps there are new factors, new variables in our equation, which invalidate all past attempts at solution. It is time we investigated this possibility.

Most obvious of new factors, new certainly within the last century, is the decrease in the size of the earth. You have all seen some of these ingenious diagrams by which the size of the earth when men had to sail or ride horseback is compared with its size when men can go in jet planes. In this sense, the world today, thanks to the airplane, is smaller than the Hellas of Pericles. Thanks to the radio, communication around the globe can be instantaneous. True enough, there remain numerous isolated and backward regions, and the actualities of modern transport and communication are not always what they seem to be in essays on the miracles of modern science. There are pockets on earth where men travel much less than 600 miles per hour. Nonetheless, ours is physically one world.

This means that no such self-isolated political unit as the Roman Empire can now exist. It will not be sufficient, though it may be helpful, to organize re-

gional federations, a United States of Europe, or a
Danubian federation. It would not be possible for a
European, an Asiatic, and an American superstate to
live in virtual separateness and self-sufficiency, as did
in the first centuries of our era the Roman and the
Chinese Empires.[1] Any arrangements for lessening the
chances of war, whether through a United Nations
held together as hardly more than an alliance or
through a genuine governmental unit with police and
taxing powers, would in our world ultimately have to
be world-wide.

This is a new factor. But I cannot believe that this
new factor makes our problem simpler, makes political
integration easier, quicker, more likely than it has
been in the past. On the contrary, I believe it makes
our problem harder. Necessity may be the mother of
invention, but surely not of perfection. Massachusetts
and Virginia were hard to bring together under a common government. France and Britain, despite the
Entente, despite the famous offer of union Churchill
made in 1940, will be hard to bring together under
a common government. Think of bringing Chinese,
Argentinians, Russians and all the other seventy-odd
"sovereign" peoples together in this way! What have
these people in common? Not religion, not language,
not tradition, not habits. They have in common only

[1] This separateness was not of course absolute. See F. J. Tag-
gart's *Rome and China* (University of California Press, 1939).

the barest, undeveloped and unfulfilled attributes of *homo sapiens.*

Perhaps even more obvious to some of you is another new factor, the atomic bomb. On this subject it is difficult, and perhaps immoral, even to try to take up an objective attitude. Nevertheless, I shall make the attempt. The first thing to be clear about is that we really do not know what effect the existence of the atomic bomb will have on the process of political integration in our world. Probably, as my friends among the physicists tell me, we can rule out the chance that the bomb in any prospective form will set off a chain-reaction among the staid, ordinary atoms that surround us, and thus actually blow this planet to bits, or at least destroy all living things on the planet. Yet we cannot rule out of our calculations the fact that a certain number of people believe this complete destruction possible, even likely, and fear it. We are dealing, not so much with a question of physics as with the question of human hopes and fears.

New books and lectures on the atomic bomb multiply daily. I cannot here pretend to take up the subject thoroughly, and were I to do so, I should distort this book. In broad lines, I think one can say that the main possibilities of the influence of the atomic bomb, as a fact and as a threat, on our contemporary problem of political integration are three. First, the bomb may in the hands of a very skillful and very lucky nation prove to be the weapon that permits that nation to unify the world by conquest, by the method of imperialism, to do what Napoleon and Hitler failed to do. Second, the bomb, especially as a threat, may so work on the fears of the many, may so inspire the crusading, intelligent few, that a successful world government will be set up federally, by the method of consent. Third, the bomb may be no more than the starting point for sermons, editorials, books, and pamphlets by prophets, crusaders, alarmists, editors, preachers, and professors, much as poison gas was last time, and have no really important effect as a variable in the equation of international politics, at least until the next world war.

Those who have followed me discerningly so far, whether in agreement or disagreement, will know that I consider this third possibility the most likely one. I incline to the belief that the atomic bomb will not greatly alter the basic problem of political integration, that it is *not* a new variable that invalidates the lessons of history. Yet I do not wish to be dogmatic. Both of the other possibilities I have mentioned seem to me to be real ones. We should all keep our minds open to new evidence in favor of either of them. Personally, I think that the bomb is more likely to promote the imperialist solution than the federal solution. Above all, if the bomb proves in the next few years to have had as its main psychological effect an increase in men's fears, then I think it clear that we shall be further than ever from the federal solution. For fear breeds distrust and aggression, not confidence and collaboration. The notion that if enough people fear they'll be blown to bits by an atomic bomb they will get together in a parliament of man is a singularly naive one. As an element in turning public opinion toward international coöperation, a reasonable fear of the consequences of atomic warfare is no doubt a factor that must be weighed in the total balance; but an obsessive fear, an overshadowing fear of the kind some of our wilder prophets apparently want to promote, seems to me one of the surest roads to war. We need not be Freudians to acknowledge the relation between anxiety and aggression.

A third new factor I see as a very real one. We can, I think, admit that some part of Marx's economic interpretation of history affords us valid uniformities about the behavior of men in society. Now it is quite true that the rise of a money-economy was incompatible with the self-sufficient feudal manor, and helped very greatly to produce the nation-state of modern times. I think it quite likely that the growth of really large-scale industry, the industrial revolution of our own times, that of the internal combustion engine, oil, electricity, the assembly-line, has made the nation-state, especially in Europe and in Latin America, a unit impossibly small for the kind of economic life that its inhabitants are trying to lead. The autarkic nation-state, unless it is a subcontinental state like Russia, Brazil, or the United States, is perhaps an economic anomaly in 1947, as the feudal lordship was in 1497.

But there is no reason why the devotees of world union *now* should take encouragement from this economic factor. In the first place, and subject always to the catastrophic potentialities of atomic warfare, the means of production under our modern neotechnical large industry needs for real efficiency either much freer international trade, or an autarkic political unit bigger than France or Peru; it does not in itself necessitate a world union. It could quite readily accommodate itself to a world of four or five independent superstates holding themselves in the kind of war-breeding balance of power we are thoroughly familiar with.

Second, we must realize that if economic necessity, or what seems to enough people to be economic necessity, is a powerful force in human affairs, this felt necessity does have to work through human beings imperfectly trained in the science of economics, and not at all likely to behave as the economist wants them to. In the long run, we human beings do perhaps adapt ourselves to material necessity. But it is a very long run, in the course of which, oddly enough, material necessity seems to get softened up, altered. If you will forgive another excursion into history, I should like to point out that the political transition from feudalism to the nation-state, though more rapid in England, say, than in Germany, everywhere took centuries, and was everywhere somewhat, and often a great deal, slower than economic change.

Third, if our sentiments and our habits cannot adapt themselves in time to the political and economic needs of large-scale industry, then it always remains possible that we shall have to abandon large-scale industry. This possibility is shocking to those brought up in the faith of the necessary progress toward bigger and better things; but it is in no way inconsonant with the record of the past.

Fourth, just as with the atomic bomb, this economic variable can be said to make the solution by imperialism at least as likely as that by federalism, perhaps more likely. We Americans are today the greatest masters of the new economic techniques. We have, perhaps, so great a comparative advantage in industrial capability over any likely combination of opponents that we might physically at least be able to conquer the world. If at any given moment a single state possesses a really great comparative advantage of this sort — and that state may not always be the USA — it may be sorely tempted to world conquest.

These three new factors, the shrinking of this earth

to county size, the invention of the atomic bomb, and the development of the techniques of modern large-scale industry, do not seem to me to invalidate what we have learned from the past of political integration. They *are* new factors, and their existence should make us more than ever cautious and tentative in making generalizations. We cannot be quite sure how they will operate. The threat of the atomic bomb may actually smooth the way to world peace. I repeat, I think such a result very unlikely, but I would not entirely close my mind to its possibility.

No doubt we could discover a great many other novel factors in the present international situation. We might, for instance, consider the chances of a widespread spiritual revolution in mankind, the advent of a new, or reborn, world religion of gentleness and love which would make all men brothers, and end war. These are delicate matters into which the objectively inquiring mind is likely to blunder awkwardly. I cannot myself really conceive such a revolution in the hearts of men as would make them gentle. At any rate, it is clear that the despairing cry, "if only they'd *try* Christianity," is not very relevant here. The Christian must, I suppose, always hope that men will shortly try to behave like Christians — or Buddhists, or Mohammedans. Until they do so behave, we shall have to go by the precedents of their past actions.

III

We have constructed, as the economists are fond of saying, a sort of "model" of a political unit made from once independent units. This new unit has a symbolic head, an administrative system possessing what is commonly called "sovereignty," an elite loyal above all to the new unit, a general population at least mildly loyal to the new unit, and sufficiently autonomous to be free from chronic and ingrowing nationalism. We have seen that it is at least very unlikely that modern scientific achievement, the pressure of economic forces, or the sudden religious conversion of mankind will build this model, or something like it, quite quickly here on earth. We must assume that the process of political integration will in the near future be not altogether unlike that process in the past.

At this point, I must enter frankly on the way of the prophet. Our first general possibility is that the work of integration will be done predominantly by the means I have called imperialist. We have seen that it is by no means inconceivable that the atomic bomb and other wonders of science would permit the quick and easy conquest of the world by a small group of determined men based almost of necessity on some existing nation-state, and probably supported by the patriotic feelings of the great mass of the inhabitants of that state. Yet on the likelihood of so melodramatic an event I remain, if not from Missouri, at least from New England, which is not a very credulous region. I promised to go against professional ethics of historians, and try to prophesy; I did not promise to try to give you science-fiction. World unity may be achieved in circumstances suited to a Buck Rogers comic strip. I am constitutionally quite unable to key my imagination to depicting such a result. It seems to me more likely that men will fight with the new weapons not too unequally, that victory will be hard won, and that a world-empire will have to be built slowly, and by political as well as by military or magical skills. I do not say a new world-empire would have to be built as slowly as that of Rome, for much has been speeded up in our time; but I do not expect such an empire to be built by a single *coup de théâtre*.

If then, world union by force must be achieved not too rapidly, and by means of force wisely guided, and helped by tolerance, organizing skill, hard work, the devotion of a trained elite, intelligent but not too intellectual — in short, by methods familiar from Roman and British history — what signs do existing nation-states show of providing such resources and such skills? What China or India, or the *united* peoples of old Europe might achieve in another future one cannot sensibly guess. At the moment, I see for the near future only three potential imperialist world-organizers, the United States, Russia, and the British

Commonwealth and Empire. Now, to come out bluntly,
I do not think that any of the three has what it takes
to do the job.

We Americans have many assets for the task, but
I do not believe we could make a *pax Americana* for
the globe. We have great energy, and we are today
as ubiquitous in the farthest corners of the world as
was once the Englishman. We have to the full the
great Anglo-Saxon gift of identifying our desires with
universal human obligations. We should never attempt, as Hitler did, to conquer crudely for our own
avowed good; when we conquer people, or indeed have
any dealings with them, we do so for their good. Please
do not think I am being cynical, or even, as is quaintly
said in authoritarian Leftist circles in America, "liberal." What shallow rationalists call hypocrisy is apparently one of the essentials of an imperial people.
One of the grave troubles with the Germans as an
imperial people is their bluntness as to their aims.
And, of course, we Americans have great wealth, a
magnificent production plant, and still abundant natural resources. Some of us, however, are beginning
to worry about these resources, and wondering if they
cannot be supplemented abroad. Of course, this desire
for other peoples' goods is initially one of the great
spurs to imperialism.

Yet I doubt whether we should make good imperialists, good enough to carry the job through to world

unity. To begin with, we are still in most ways a democracy, and democracies in the past have never proven to be good at building empires. They cannot, apparently, pursue for long enough a consistent policy toward other peoples; they cannot provide the right sort of imperial administrations. But these are abstract considerations. I think I get nearer the heart of the matter if I say that I just don't feel my countrymen have the stuff of imperialists. Our armies in this war, though they did well the job they had to do, were surely the most homesick of armies. The lad who went through Britain, France, Italy or New Guinea bemoaning the absence of the corner drugstore seems to me no fit successor to the Roman legionary. Again, though as a people we have grave failures from the standpoint of any high ethical and aesthetic codes ever devised, though, for instance, many American boys overseas in this war treated the inhabitants of foreign countries with amused contempt, nonetheless there remains as a basis of the American character a willingness to live and let live, a pathetic desire for a world in which nobody is pushed about. Perhaps I am trying to say that there is a rather profound emotional sense in which Americans really are believers in democracy. At any rate, there has to be a deal of pushing about to found a world-empire, and I don't believe we'll do it.

As for the Russians, I shall have to confess that I

have no inside information, and no really profound first-hand acquaintance with the Russian people. I have to struggle — though frankly I don't know why I should struggle — against a tendency to believe the truth to be the opposite, the antipodean opposite, of whatever appears in the Hearst or the McCormick press. Since these vicious newspapers have for several years been telling me that the Russians intend to try to conquer the world, I naturally incline to believe that the Russians have no such intention. But I suppose it is conceivable that even such as Mr. Hearst and Colonel McCormick may occasionally be right. I have been trying awfully hard in this discussion to be open-minded and objective, so I suppose we can stretch a point, and envision truth in relation with Messrs. Hearst and McCormick.

Grant then to the Russians the *will* to try for world conquest. They have still a good deal of technological inferiority to overcome, and that is bound to take time. They have, however, a broad territorial base, rich in natural resources, a growing and active population, a national pride and energy greatly enhanced by their successful stand against the Germans. They are not handicapped for the imperialist struggle by the kind of habits and institutions we Americans associate with democracy. They have given proof of ability to organize in the unity of the Union of Socialist Soviet Republics a considerable number and variety of peoples and nationalities. In fact, the present USSR represents in itself a very considerable achievement in political integration.

Yet, again, I cannot see our world organized under a *pax Russica*. I do not really believe the Russian people are prepared to make the sacrifices, to acquire the conditioning, necessary for such an imperial achievement. The aggressiveness, even the megalomania, often shown by some of their leaders seem to me in part the inevitable or at any rate customary bluster of competitive international politics, in part, as any psychiatrist can tell you, a mask for anxiety and fear, fear above all of us and of our atomic bomb. But I prefer not to rest my case on a statement so controversial as that the Russians don't want to conquer the world, but do want to be secure. I should like to bring forward two more obviously valid reasons why I do not think the Russians will make successful world conquerors. The first is psychological. It is not so much a matter of the celebrated and inefficient Slavic soul — that I think contemporary Russians have pretty well lived down — but rather one of simple getting on with other peoples, or at least not rousing their hatreds. Here I see good signs that the Russians, like the Germans, are not only unable to make themselves loved by other peoples — as a matter of fact, one people probably never does love another people — but are unable to make themselves at all acceptable to other peoples. And remember that one thing is very clear from our historical record: mere force is not enough. A successful imperial people must be acceptable to those it rules. Second, I believe that the Russian commitment to a new religion, that of Communism, is on the whole a handicap to any Russian attempt to build a world-empire, or even a world-state under her own hegemony. Communism has already roused religious hatreds against itself, and these hatreds reinforce whatever opposition Russia as a political entity in the rivalry of international politics would naturally rouse. What therefore may seem to the hopes of the convert to Communism or to the fears of the worried conservative a source of strength in Russia, that is, the Russian espousal of the cause of the proletariat, seems to me a source of weakness. I think it clear by now that, however the unity of the world is to be achieved, it will not come because the proletarians of the world unite.

On the possibility that the already very great agglomeration of lands and peoples known as the British Commonwealth and Empire — it is roughly one quarter of the earth's land and people — might imperialistically absorb the rest of the world, I can be briefer. The British have displayed what can only be called at least a Roman aptitude for empire. But the core of their Empire, the British Isles, has been reduced by two world wars in close succession to a point where it can hardly support the strain of further expansion. I am not among those who believe the British are done for, but I do not think they are capable of bringing the whole world, including Russia and these United States, under a *pax Britannica*. Their great self-governing dominions are too widely scattered and too thinly populated to support the task of helping their motherland conquer the rest of the world, even if they wanted to do it. India, statistically the source of most of the imposing figures for the British agglomeration, is certainly no foundation stone of empire at the present moment. We need hardly pursue this matter further.

There remains the greatest threat, or if you prefer, the greatest promise. This is an Anglo-American combination to rule the world through a *pax Anglo-Americana*. I can conceive such a combination, if it were made effective, having quite the best stab at world domination in modern times, quite a bit better than those of Charles V, Louis XIV, Napoleon, and Hitler. I think, however, for reasons I shall come to shortly, that even this attempt would fail. But I do not think there is the slightest chance that it will be made. That there are a few British and a few Americans who have dreamed and still dream of a world benignly ruled by English-speaking peoples, clean, honest, and practically blond, it would be foolish to deny. Could the most effective possible Anglo-American imperial elite be formed, and could it work in harmony, it might well push the rest of us Americans and British into this more than Rhodesian attempt. But the great mass of Americans and British are in no mood for such adventures, and seem unlikely in the foreseeable future to attain such a mood. Specific union of some sort between the two countries, or the reduction of Great Britain to the status of Commonwealth in an *American* Commonwealth and Empire, would seem to be essential to any Anglo-American world rule. And while legislators still talk, and finally vote, on Capitol Hill and in Westminster, I think such union impossible. Finally, we must remember that the rest of the world would have a voice in the establishment of a *pax Anglo-Americana*. Quantitatively quite a voice, for even today only about one human being in ten is English-speaking.

This brings me to my firmest reason for not believing that the method of imperialism will be successful within a predictable future. In our modern past, in the five hundred years of the nation-state, no one power has ever got dominance for the simple reason that sooner or later the other powers, big, middle-sized, and little, all ganged up against the aggressor, and eventually defeated him. Sooner or later against the most powerful aggressor a coalition is formed, and in the long run this coalition is too strong for the aggressor.[2] Now, in spite of loose talk about there being only two real powers left on this earth, the USA and the USSR, it is clear that there are still seventy-odd nation-states. Should the United States, or the Russians, or the British attempt world conquest by force, I confidently expect that the other nations would line up with whichever powers seemed least aggressive, least a threat to their own independence. And, in this world, if not in Buck Rogers's, I should expect this coalition to beat the aggressive superpower. I know this is history, and I feel it is common sense.

IV

If there is little prospect of world unity by the method of imperialism, may there not be greater prospect of such unity by the method of federalism? I think there is a somewhat greater prospect of unity by this method, though I should be dishonest with myself were I to maintain here that I think world unity through federalism likely in our time.

A few months ago I was leading a discussion group among wounded veterans in a Massachusetts hospital. I was expressing my doubts as to the success in our time of the movement for world federation, when one of the men remarked, "Oh, yes, Mr. Brinton, I know

[2] I cannot resist referring here to my attempt to apply this line of reasoning at the beginning of this last war: Crane Brinton, "Napoleon and Hitler," *Foreign Affairs*, January, 1942.

people of your temperament. Had you been in Philadelphia in 1787 you would have said that of course the
efforts of the Constitutional Convention were doomed
in advance to failure." What that veteran said certainly bit into my conscience, but I still am unable to
believe that the task facing world federationists today
and the task facing Franklin, Hamilton, Madison, and
the others at Philadelphia in 1787 are really comparable. We Americans had in 1787 one language, one
law, one cultural tradition, with no more than the sort
of provincial differences that separated Boston, Philadelphia, and Charleston; we had worked together as a
going concern, as a team, in spite of our quarrels, ever
since the first Continental Congress. The nation-states
of 1948 have no such common linguistic, legal, or cultural inheritance; they have just fought two major
wars among themselves; and their brief and incomplete union in the League of Nations is hardly comparable to our Congress. The League was very little
more than a form of the balance of power.

Moreover, praise though you may the skill and wis-
dom of the men who assembled at Philadelphia, weigh
heavily if you will as a superb job of propaganda the
famous *Federalist Papers,* you cannot really maintain
that the current movement for world federation is in
any part of the world in a position at all comparable
to that of the proponents of our federal Constitution
of 1787–1789. In this country, men like Mr. Justice

Roberts, Mr. Clarence Streit, Mr. Grenville Clark, Mr. Robert Humber, Mr. Emery Reves, and Mr. Cord Meyer, able, inspired, and virtuous though they undoubtedly are, are simply not in a position to get things done as were Franklin, Jefferson, Washington, Hamilton, Madison, Jay, and the other Founding Fathers. Historically, real federal unions have been relatively few, hard to establish, and limited to groups which already possessed much, and that much positive, not a mere negative like fear, in common.

The American Constitution, moreover, was ultimately established by the active consent of the people of the thirteen states. It was indeed produced by an elite, and to a certain extent made acceptable to the people by the prestige and the political skill of this elite. No one of course supposes that the peoples of this earth, all the twenty-two thousand million, could assemble and will themselves a world-state. There will have to be leaders, an elite. But the ultimate decision *under the method of federalism* will have to be made by the peoples; and even if you rule out black Africans and Polynesians, you can hardly rule out Chinese, Japanese, and East Indians. In other words, you will need not only the eventual allegiance of the masses to the world-state — as I noted in the first chapter, I think the Roman superstate did not really secure the allegiance of the masses — but you will have to have their initial and active acceptance of the world federation. You will have, in American, to sell them a constitution. Can you really imagine a new *Federalist* winning over the Chinese, the Arabs, the Russians, and the Americans? Can you really conceive such acceptance from the Americans who only twenty-odd years ago balked at Article 10 of the League Covenant? Can you see how the Russian people would go about accepting, supposing that they wanted to? Would you get the Jews and the Arabs to lie down together peacefully even in a parliament of man? Who will sign acceptance for Spain? for China? I give these horrendous concrete difficulties, not out of a spirit of contrariousness, but because these difficulties are there, now, in 1948.

If you think of the human passions, the human habits, all of what Mark Twain called the "damned human race," lying behind these concrete difficulties, I think you will not have the temerity to call them ephemeral difficulties. They, and their like, are in our times permanent difficulties. They, and their like, in our times make the attainment of a world-state by the method of federal union impossible. "Impossible," Napoleon is said to have said, "is not a French word." That is not, by the way, one of the remarks he made at St. Helena; he must have made it rather before the retreat from Moscow. Impossible is of course a most human word in every language. We use it of undignified matters, like gardening, and say quite readily that it is impossible to grow oranges outdoors in our time in New England. Why can we not use it of dignified matters, like morals and politics, and say that in our time a United States of the World is impossible?

V

Yet I should not like to close this book on so pessimistic a note. After all, if we cannot grow oranges in New England we can, no matter what New York City novelists may say, grow many things there. In many sorts of human activities, such as gardening, farming, perhaps most of the duller business of life, we are really conditioned to working with recalcitrant, complex, perverse materials that won't behave just as we want them to behave. One might even say that most of us as parents in relation to our children realize we are working with such materials. The materials out of which someday world peace may be made are at least as difficult, as complicated, as perverse as those with which we struggle in our daily problems. Because the questions of international order seem to us remote, abstract, grand, we ought not to think them more easily, more idealistically, solvable than our little ones, which we never quite solve, never quite expect to solve, and yet, while we keep out of the madhouse, never quite give up trying to solve.

I think the immediate future, then, will see no world-state established either by the method of imperialism or by the method of federalism. I should expect the present world-system of seventy-odd nation-states to continue in a precarious equilibrium, known historically as a balance of power, until some such aggression as the last two German ones broke the balance. Judging from the past of the system, I should not expect this new aggression to reach the active stage of provoking a new war on a world scale before thirty or forty years, and perhaps even longer. But concrete prediction here is very risky, as in the somewhat similar task of predicting the business cycle in a world of imperfect economic planning (and perhaps even in a world of perfect economic planning). The United Nations I regard as a possibly very effective palliative of war and as a means of lengthening the spells of actual peace; and though this may seem to the more enthusiastic faint praise indeed, I mean it to be very real praise. At any rate, the United Nations is like a spray which we've got to keep using; we may not even then get perfect fruit, indeed we shan't get perfect fruit, but we ought to get a crop.

In the long pull, I see certain encouraging signs. I have throughout this book endeavored to follow the dry light of science, and avoid those more generous speculations of the imaginative prophets of our day, the Toynbees, the Sorokins, the Spenglers, the Rosenstock-Huessys, and other philosophers of history. I have tried not to generalize beyond the evidence. You will then perhaps forgive me if I nibble just once in the green pastures of the imagination. It seems possible that what Arnold Toynbee calls "universal states" — that is, the end product of what I have called here the process of political integration — are, or at any rate have been, signs of death and disintegration of cultures. I cannot here go into this fascinating problem, and can only suggest that the Roman Empire, which I have here taken as an achievement in political integration, may be taken as a form of human and cultural disintegration. The wrangling Lilliputian states of fifth-century Hellas have seemed to many sensitive moderns alive in a sense that Rome was never alive. Our Victorian grandfathers, indeed, who had little direct experience of such competition in the form of war, tended to regard competition among independent political units, such as nation-states, as a source of life-giving evolutionary energy.

We cannot in 1948, it seems to me, consider the competitive nation-state system a desirable thing in itself. Some form of political integration transcending the sovereign nation-state seems to me personally an almost inevitable purpose for all who still cherish the generous hopes with which this country was founded. We may hope ultimately to do better than the Romans, if we can have the patience — and if the scientists and inventors will let us exercise the patience — to try to transcend the nation-state by the method of consent. For may not the answer to those who associate universal states with the decline of human energy and human culture be that universal states in the past have been put together initially by force, not by consent, and that they have never recovered from the wounds they received at their birth? Can we perhaps meet successfully the challenge men have rarely if ever met before, the challenge to make of many one without destroying the many?

There are certain indications that we human beings are slowly improving relations among nation-states. The progress is modest, so modest as to seem negligible to the confirmed idealist, and to all who habitually accept that deadliest of formulas: "either . . . or." But at the conclusion of almost every one of the recent world wars, in 1713, in 1815, in 1918, and in 1945, a more explicit, more concrete, more far-reaching, and in many senses more successful attempt to set up machinery for international consultation to maintain peace has been made. Only the settlement of 1763 is an apparent exception here. But from the Congresses of Cambrai and of Soissons, so bitterly ridiculed by Carlyle in his *Frederick the Great,* through Vienna and Versailles to the Conference of San Francisco there is evident most clearly what less disillusioned people than ourselves would have called simply "progress."

Again, there is the slow growth of international law.

I know that some of the clear-minded, who are often also the simple-minded, insist that where there is no authority to make law there is no law possible, and that since there is no international authority there is no international law. I shall not here pick a quarrel with these people. I shall merely say that it seems to me that law is at least as much a product of human desires and of human habits as of human commands, and that there has been some kind of international law ever since there were international relations. What has come out of Nuremberg seems to me again, in innocent language, progress in international law.

There is clearly, though again slowly, being formed an international elite. In one sense, modern Europe has never wholly lacked such an elite. In the early eighteenth-century, and largely under French cultural influence, cosmopolitan administrators and intellectuals seemed almost on the point of restoring at least the kind of cultural unity Europe had in the Middle Ages. Their work was largely destroyed by the romantic nationalists of the next century. Nowadays, in the working bodies of the League of Nations and its successor the United Nations, in the churches, in the universities and the learned foundations, in the press, even in the more extreme pressure groups, such as the world federationists I have been faintly and ambiguously damning, yes, even in the chancelleries of professional diplomacy, even in departments of State, there is growing a group of men and women skilled in the ways of coöperation among varied peoples, trained and practiced persons, an international elite not entirely divorced from national allegiance, but on the whole devoted to the task of getting in practice beyond the sovereign nation-state. This elite has not yet all the characteristics we found in other international elites. Notably these people have not yet a common language — and, parenthetically, I cannot believe that language will be English, if only because the language will have to be spelled as well as spoken — and they have no such common faith as the Stoics had. They are perhaps too sharply divided into the hard-boiled and the soft-boiled, and there are not enough just properly set. The proportion of preachers and teachers among them may still be a bit excessive. They probably form too much of a coterie, if not a sect, who see too much of one another at meetings, conferences, congresses, and other places where the converted preach to the converted. But they exist, and to me their existence is a sign of progress.

They do not, as a matter of fact, wholly preach to the converted; they do make converts — subject, like all converts, to occasional backsliding. No one who remembers 1918 can doubt that there has been in this country a vast increase in public interest in foreign affairs. There are no doubt many reasons why, after refusing to join the League of Nations, we now find ourselves a charter member of the United Nations. But one of the chief reasons is surely that the American people are beginning to try to understand their place in the world, to try to implement their firm desire for peace. In Britain and in France the story is the same. We have throughout the world the beginnings, perhaps only the faint beginnings, of the kind of mass interest and mass participation in the affairs of the world without which precedent would indicate no lasting world order is possible. I know you will not accuse me of innocent idealism. We have a very long way to go before we can get the participation of the common man in a common thing greater than the nation-state as we know it. Even in Britain, where the people are perhaps the most internationally minded of any, John Smith and Jack Jones are certainly more interested in the Football Cup, the Oaks or the Ashes, than they are in international relations. But again, there is in public opinion all over the world a foundation, a beginning, something on which we can all get to work.

How far regional federations promote world peace is difficult to say. Four or five superstates could, and probably would, quarrel as badly as have the miscellaneous dozens of today, or hundreds of yesterday, or thousands of ancient times. Perhaps there is a certain naïveté in holding that the reduction of the states of South America or of Europe by federation would be a step toward world unity. Yet I incline to believe that some such federations are in fact a necessary step on the long road to world unity, that only by bringing together states closely allied by tradition (even if like that of France and England it is a tradition of hostility), by geographic and economic conditions, by a certain similarity of culture, can we test the capacity of the human race to unite. On the whole, we human beings usually in practice do quite strongly prefer to attempt the easier thing before the harder thing, even though such a choice may seem inglorious, and is not approved by our more idealistic spiritual leaders.

I need hardly add that science and technology can help build international peace, and that they can help destroy it. Rapid transportation and communications can help solve the problems they have so largely served to raise. But their use depends on the heads and hearts of the men who use them. There are no machines that can, by themselves, promote the process of political integration — nor, I believe, wholly and catastrophically destroy the possibility of such integration. Even the atomic bomb remains an instrument within the scope of human purpose; its force is the force of human will.

We have, then, seen signs that the goal of ending war among territorial units by the establishment of some sort of world government is, very distantly, to be glimpsed by the eye of faith. I cannot believe the goal so near that there will be no war between us and it. I cannot, therefore, believe that those extremists who go about insisting that there can and hence must never be another war, that we must have world government immediately or be blown to bits, are doing the least good. Indeed, I fear that to the extent that plain people take these extremists seriously, the world federationists are doing harm. But, finally, I do not think plain people do take the extremists, the idealists, the "either . . . or" folk, seriously. No one has yet called this last one the "war to end war." We human beings are perhaps rather silly animals, rather stupid ones, but we are also very tough ones; men, women and children of our great and supposedly effete European cities stood up under months of bombardment, though the Italian military prophet Guilio Douhet had before the war written confidently that no civilian population could stand forty-eight hours of air attacks. And we are very persistent animals; we go on spraying, oranges or apples, California or New England, year after year without a ray of hope that we can ever totally eliminate insect pests and fungi, and so not ever again have to spray. Some of our scientists may cherish such hopes, but they have not contaminated the workers in the field. Some of our social scientists may cherish the hope that they can find a way to prevent war ever again breaking out, but they clearly have not contaminated the workers in the field. I cannot really believe that even atomic war will finish so tough an organism as man.

CONCLUSION

CONCLUSION

I have tried in these chapters to preach no more than seems unavoidable in any study of human relations. I have tried to keep my own feelings from asserting themselves noisily and obviously. Perhaps I shall be forgiven if in this brief conclusion I preach frankly. I trust I preach out of my experience of the objective and dispassionate study of human behavior in the past and in the present; but if I fail in this, and preach out of my own unanalyzed hopes and fears, I shall be in the very best company.

To put the matter in indecent brevity: many — indeed probably most — politically and morally interested and self-conscious Europeans, and especially most such Americans, accept emotionally and intellectually some form of belief in progress and human perfectability here on earth. This belief ripened in the Age of Enlightenment, the eighteenth century in which our own United States was born. This belief persists in spite of attacks from many quarters, and in spite of the obvious fact that human behavior, human "arrangements," are no better now — many intellectuals would say they are worse — than they were two centuries ago. The belief has, we are told, weakened somewhat in Europe these last few years; but most literate Americans still hold that human behavior, human arrangements, can be made markedly better very quickly. I do not say that we as a people believe that Utopia is just around the corner; but we do at least have a tendency to believe that under certain conditions (notably if a law is passed) life on this earth can be made a lot rosier for everybody, and in fairly short time. How far this optimism has penetrated into the hearts and minds of ordinary, non-intellectual Americans is a hard question. At least among American intellectuals, among teachers, preachers, improvers, agitators, planners and the like, belief in the rapid alteration of human behavior by alteration in laws, treaties, education, and propaganda is very strong. And contrary to American folk-notions, these intellectuals, even the special kind called in this country "liberals," probably have a very great influence on the fate of the United States and of the world.

The late James Harvey Robinson, an American liberal, a historian, and an admirable writer, is here an excellent example. He was fully aware of all that two centuries of experience had brought against the basic thesis of the Enlightenment: the thesis of the natural goodness and reasonableness of man. He had even read Pareto, and was probably the first well-known American writer to refer to the Sociologie générale. *Robinson thought man still an animal, with animal appetites and animal inability to think rationally. He wrote a book,* Mind in the Making, *in which he pointed out carefully what a slow process organic evolution had been, how long it had taken man to struggle up from the ape. He pointed out how little different we are, not only from the Greeks of two thousand years ago, but from the cave men of twenty thousand years ago. In the immense course of geological time, the whole development of* homo sapiens *is but a few fleeting moments. H. G. Wells did much the same thing, and with much the same message, in his* Outline of History.

Both these liberals, men of the very best will, insist that the record of the past shows that even men, even human institutions, apparently change very slowly indeed. And then both come to the conclusion that mankind is at the crossroads, that it is later than we think, that we face "either . . . or" in its starkest form, that we must suddenly transform ourselves into better men, or at the very least, into good practicing liberals, or mankind will perish at its own hands. It has taken us eons to get this far, and yet the next stage must be made at a dizzy speed. There is behind this insistence on a new rate of change no very clear notion of how such change can come about. Robinson is perhaps as clear as any. He seems to believe that, though most of us still carry the weight of centuries of animal appetites, prejudices, fears, so that even when we try to think we think unclearly, nevertheless, once we are properly taught, and realize our errors, we can think straight. A straight thinker — or rather, millions of them together — would never put up with anything less than world peace.

Now I submit that Wells and Robinson were quite right about their time-scale, and quite wrong to abandon it when they came to the present and the near future. The kind of change which our reformers want may not be impossible, but there is every evidence that this sort of change in human behavior has always been very slow indeed, almost as slow as the kind of change the geologist and the paleontologist study. Science provides no evidence that the time-scale of human change has altered, and it really is absurd for men like Wells and Robinson to claim from science support for their hopes of a miracle. Again, let me make clear that I do not deny the possibility that the miracle of universal peace may be brought about in this world now. But such a miracle would simply lie outside the scope of what we call science, and of what we call liberalism. It would be wholly inside the scope of what we call religion.

When our modern prophets like Wells and Robinson go back to pithecanthropus erectus *and further, when they lay claim to scientific basis for their dreams of peace on earth, they are putting on a false front. They are, in fact, people of the sort I shall call perfectionists, and they belong in the company of the Hebrew prophets, Plato, the more evangelical Chris-*

tians, the idealists, the whole-hog reformers, the revolutionists of the spirit. As I have already said, I cannot understand the idealist in a hurry; indeed I probably cannot understand the idealist. I used in my last chapter, and somewhat despairingly, an analogy turning on an attempt to grow oranges outdoors in New England. To me, Plato was all his life trying to grow oranges outdoors in a sub-freezing temperature. To me, the world federationists are trying to do the same thing. This is a confession which may exclude me from the fellowship of men of depth and imagination. But I shall summon the courage of my shallowness.

In hardly any other kind of human activity do men behave as do the perfectionists in their dealing with moral, political, social, economic problems, with human relations, in short. Indeed, the perfectionists themselves, unless they are Bronson Alcotts, usually manage to compromise with this world in matters like eating, drinking, raising a family, and so on. To come back to my first analogy: men have not stood still in orange-growing; far from it, they have immensely improved the cultivation of that fruit. Indeed, the scientist, technician, and inventor in combination have often achieved the impossible — by not attempting the impossible. Only in human relations do we frankly, virtuously, and a bit monotonously attempt the impossible — or at any rate, try to persuade others to let us attempt it. On my own grounds, I suppose I should admit that since the perfectionists have persisted ever since we have any record (Amenophis IV — Ikhnaton — was surely one of them, a thousand years before Plato) they must play a useful role in society. Perhaps they do. But at the moment I, too, am preaching.

I suggest that the people I have called perfectionists do more harm than good on this earth, and that they ought to be combatted, not embraced as allies, by all who hope to further the good life on this earth. I mean here no Nietzschean transvaluation of values. The perfectionists and I are in pretty complete agreement as to ends, as to what the good life on this earth might be. But we differ as to means. We agree as to what health is, and we want the patient's health to be as good as possible; we differ as to the nature, length, and completeness of the possible cure. I do not think that there is any full cure for the human race on this earth.

Traditional Christianity does not believe that there is any such cure on this earth either. How far the masses in our Western society are in this respect still Christians is a question of very great importance which I do not think can at present be answered. With all our Gallup polls and other testing, we still know a lot more about the intellectuals than about the unin-tellectuals. I am fairly sure that even in the United States the uneducated and unspeculative majority never did put their whole faith in the New Heaven on earth. I suspect that even now, though the common man in this country wants world peace, he does not really expect to get it.

The intellectuals, however, the bright young people growing up to take over leadership in this world, the active, interested people who try to get things done in their own communities, the people who read and talk about foreign affairs — these very important and, all told, numerous people, whom I hesitate to call an elite for fear of offending them, are, I think, unduly influenced by the perfectionists. They are in danger of falling into the trap of "either . . . or" which is the favorite device of the perfectionist. They have been told so often that we must have world peace or perish that they may have come to believe this a real dilemma. They will be even more bewildered by the next war than we were by this, and even less ready for it.

But the generation of British lads who swore they would not fight for King and Country lived to die for King and Country, and perhaps even in some measure for the perfectionists? Certainly, and I am not a prophet of doom even with respect to the future of the young men who will now take nothing less than a world-state. I think they will come through an atomic war. But they will come through it very painfully, and they will be unnecessarily scarred by it, if they believe it quite impossible. They may even, I fear, bring it on a bit sooner and more disastrously if they try in the perfectionists' way to avoid it. The young Britishers of the thirties are not a happy augury.

I am not making the conventional argument for military preparedness for the United States, though I do not believe that argument loses force because it is a conventional one. Nor am I repeating the commonplace, "if you wish for peace, prepare for war," though I do not believe that commonplace is as false as the pacifists think it is. I am trying to go deeper and further, into the underlying emotional basis of the beliefs we have inherited from the Age of the Enlightenment. The problem of world peace is merely the problem on which at the moment this belief is most clearly centered. Briefly, some of us, perhaps most of us, have been brought up to believe that here and now, if only enough of us try hard enough, we can get signed, sealed, and delivered the perfect instrument that will banish suffering from this earth. In an analogy which I know oversimplifies as badly as any analogy of orange-growing, but which will have to do: some of us hope for Heaven, and fear Hell, here, soon, and on earth. This is heretical to the Christian, absurd to the scientist, implausible to men of common sense, unlovely to men of imagination. One wonders to what queer part of us human beings such a hope and such a fear can appeal. Perhaps the human part?